# MAKING THE MOST
## OF THE **WEB** IN YOUR
# Classroom

### A TEACHER'S GUIDE TO BLOGS, PODCASTS, WIKIS, PAGES, AND SITES

**Timothy D. Green** ● **Abbie Brown** ● **LeAnne Robinson**

**CORWIN PRESS**
A SAGE Company
Thousand Oaks, CA 91320

*For information:*

Corwin Press
A SAGE Company
2455 Teller Road
Thousand Oaks, CA 91320
www.corwinpress.com

SAGE Ltd.
1 Oliver's Yard
55 City Road
London EC1Y 1SP
United Kingdom

SAGE India Pvt. Ltd.
B 1/I 1 Mohan Cooperative
    Industrial Area
Mathura Road, New Delhi 110 044
India

SAGE Asia-Pacific
    Pte. Ltd.
33 Pekin Street #02–01
Far East Square
Singapore 048763

Printed in the United States of America.

*Library of Congress Cataloging-in-Publication Data*

Green, Timothy D., 1968-
Making the most of the Web in your classroom : a teacher's guide to
blogs, podcasts, wikis, pages, and sites / Timothy D. Green, Abbie Brown,
LeAnne Robinson.
        p. cm.
Includes bibliographical references and indexes.
ISBN 978-1-4129-1573-1 (cloth)
ISBN 978-1-4129-1574-8 (pbk.)
    1. Web-based instruction. 2. Internet in education. 3. World Wide Web—Study and
teaching. I. Brown, Abbie. II. Robinson, LeAnne. III. Title.

LB1044.87.G74 2008
371.33′44678—dc22                    2007029940

This book is printed on acid-free paper.

07   08   09   10   11   10   9   8   7   6   5   4   3   2   1

| | |
|---|---|
| *Acquisitions Editor:* | Debra Stollenwerk |
| *Editorial Assistants:* | Jordan Barbakow, Allison Scott |
| *Production Editor:* | Jenn Reese |
| *Copy Editor:* | Trey Thoelcke |
| *Typesetter:* | C&M Digitals (P) Ltd. |
| *Proofreader:* | Victoria Reed-Castro |
| *Indexer:* | Nara Wood |
| *Cover Designer:* | Monique Hahn |

# Contents

# Preface

*"The Internet is perhaps the most transformative technology in history, reshaping business, media, entertainment, and society in astonishing ways. But for all its power, it is just now being tapped to transform education."*

*The Power of the Internet for Learning:*
*Moving From Promise to Practice*
(Web-Based Education Commission, 2000)

**W**e need to start out by admitting that we love the Web. Despite how sad or corny that may sound, it's true. We use the Web to shop, read the news, and share photos of our pets or our recent car purchases with friends and family around the world; the list could go on and on, but you get the point—we love the Web! It's hard for us to imagine how we once functioned without it.

In addition to using the Web for personal use, we use the Web professionally for research and teaching. The Web provides us with a wealth of opportunities for enhancing our curriculum and the teaching and learning that takes place in our classrooms. It is our belief that the Web can also help you enhance what you do in the classroom to assist your students to learn content and meet standards. This is why we have written this book.

Whether you are new to the wonders of the Web or you're an experienced Web surfer, we believe this book is for you. *Making the Most of the Web in Your Classroom: A Teacher's Guide to Blogs, Podcasts, Wikis, Pages, and Sites* is an all-in-one resource to help you make sense of the Web by providing guidance on what the Web is and how to use it effectively in the classroom. This book provides a blend of both technical and practical information that will help you build your knowledge base as you explore how the Web works, and how it can be integrated into your curriculum. We have written this book based on our practical knowledge and experience as classroom teachers, teacher educators, and Web designers.

The book is organized into four chapters. The first chapter is an overview of the Web. It briefly explains what the Web is and how it originated. We move on to a discussion on what makes the Web an effective tool to help enhance student learning and why teachers implement Web-based projects into the curriculum to help enhance student learning. The chapter concludes with descriptions of seven cutting-edge Web-based tools we believe every teacher should know. Although the text does not specifically focus on these tools, we believe teachers should be informed enough about the tools so they can understand what the tools are designed to accomplish. The goal of Chapter 1 is to introduce the tools and provide you with resources you can explore if you are interested in knowing more about those tools. Chapter 1 contains a number of highlighted *Curriculum Integration Ideas* as well as *Curriculum Resources* intended to help you incorporate the Web into your instructional planning.

Chapter 2 is the heart of the book. This chapter focuses on the integration of Web-based projects into the curriculum. We provide numerous examples of how teachers at various grade levels and content areas have integrated Web-based projects into their curriculum. We strived to include a variety of examples. Our hope is that by seeing these examples (and trying a few out in your classroom) you will be inspired to search for other Web-based projects and to create your own! Included in the chapter is the concept of assessment and how it fits with using the Web in the curriculum. Chapter 2 also contains a number of *Curriculum Resources* intended to help you implement, manage, and evaluate Web-based activities.

For those wanting to create their own Web-based learning activities and projects (we hope that after reading Chapter 2 this will be you!), Chapter 3 provides you with the tools to accomplish this. This chapter provides a process for successfully designing and developing Web sites. The chapter gives an introduction to HTML—the language of the Web—and how basic Web sites are physically created. Introductions to both basic coding and using HTML editors to create Web sites are provided. The chapter concludes with a discussion on elements that make for attractive and easy-to-read Web sites.

Chapter 4 is an overview of various challenges and considerations that teachers should understand and keep in mind as they integrate the Web in the classroom. Topics such as copyright, fair use, netiquette, and student safety are discussed. We believe this chapter will help teachers avoid common pitfalls that are associated with integrating the Web in the classroom.

In addition to the book, we have developed a companion Web site (http://www.drtimgreen.com/) that provides links to various Web-based resources on topics covered in the book. We hope that this resource will allow you to explore in more depth the various topics covered in the book.

## Acknowledgments

We'd like to acknowledge Robb Clouse and Deb Stollenwerk at Corwin Press for helping us make this book a reality. We appreciate their guidance through the process. We'd like to also thank the reviewers who provided us with feedback and suggestions that help shape the book.

Corwin Press would like to thank the following individuals for their contributions:

Michael Todd Edwards
Assistant Professor, Mathematics Education
Miami University
Oxford, OH

Chuck Perkins
Consulting Teacher, Explorer Academy
South Kitsap School District
Port Orchard, WA

Frank M. Betts, CEO
Rural Schools Network
Redstone, CO

Elizabeth Alvarez
CPS Area 10 Math/Science Coach
Chicago Public Schools
Chicago, IL

April Keck DeGennaro
Fayette County Schools
Gifted Education
Peeples Elementary School
Fayetteville, GA

Douglas Bailer
Earnest Pruett Center of Technology, Science and Technology Teacher
Walden University, Master's Program Instructor
Dutton, AL

Beverly Plein
Technology Resource Specialist
Benjamin Franklin Middle School
Glen Rock, NJ

Katie Morrow
Fifth-Grade Teacher
O'Neill Public Schools
O'Neill, NE

Margo Shirley
Curriculum Technology Specialist, Elementary Grades
Jordan School District
Sandy, UT

Sandra Enger
Associate Professor of Science Education
University of Alabama at Huntsville
Institute for Science Education
Huntsville, AL

Ron Wahlen
Executive Director of Instructional Technology
Durham Public Schools
Durham, NC

# About the Authors

 **Timothy D. Green**: Tim is an Associate Professor at California State University, Fullerton, in the Department of Elementary and Bilingual Education. His PhD is in Instructional Systems Technology and Curriculum and Instruction from Indiana University. He is a former fourth grade and junior high teacher. Tim has authored *PowerPoint Made Very Easy*, and he is the coauthor of *The Essentials of Instructional Design: Connecting Fundamental Principles With Process and Practice, Technology, and the Diverse Learner: A Guide to Classroom Practice*, and *Multimedia Projects in the Classroom: A Guide to Development and Evaluation*.

 **Abbie Brown**: Abbie is an Associate Professor in East Carolina University's Department of Library Science and Instructional Technology. He holds a PhD in Instructional Systems Technology from Indiana University and an MA from Teachers College at Columbia University. He has taught at the Bank Street School for Children in New York City and George Washington Middle School in Ridgewood, New Jersey, and has received awards for his outstanding teaching and curriculum design from the New Jersey Department of Education. He is coauthor of *The Essentials of Instructional Design: Connecting Fundamental Principles With Process and Practice, Technology, and the Diverse Learner: A Guide to Classroom Practice*, and *Multimedia Projects in the Classroom: A Guide to Development and Evaluation*. He is also a contributing author to *Teaching Strategies: A Guide to Effective Instruction*.

**LeAnne Robinson**: LeAnne is an Associate Professor at Western Washington University, on a joint appointment between the Program in Instructional Technology and Department of Special Education. She is a former elementary and special education teacher, and holds a PhD in Education from Washington State University. LeAnne's work has appeared in such journals as *Teaching Exceptional Children*, the *International Journal of Information and Communication Technology Education*, and *Voices in the Middle*.

# The Wide World of the Web

*Fitting It Into the Curriculum*

## GUIDING QUESTIONS

This chapter will help you answer the following questions:

- Why use the Web in my classroom?
- How does a Web project fit into my curriculum?
- What skills do I need to have?
- What are the NETS standards?
- What is the connection between the teaching and learning cycle, Universal Design for Learning, and Web projects?
- What qualities make Web projects successful learning experiences for students?
- What Web tools can I implement into my curriculum?

## KEY TERMS

Asynchronous

Blogs

Course Management/
   Learning Management
   Systems

Digital Natives

Instant Messaging

ISTE

NETS-S

NETS-T

| | |
|---|---|
| Open Source | Synchronous |
| Podcasts | Teaching and Learning Cycle |
| RSS | Universal Design for Learning |
| Social Spaces | Wikis |

## OVERVIEW

The Web has tremendous potential as a tool that can help students learn content, develop skills, and meet standards. For many teachers, meaningfully integrating the Web into the curriculum can be a daunting task. Although it may seem overwhelming at first, it's not impossible. We believe that integrating the Web into the teaching and learning process can actually become quite exciting if you spend some time exploring what the Web is, how it works, and what makes it an effective learning tool. This chapter helps you begin your exploration of the Web. The chapter explains how the Web can fit into your curriculum through the integration of various Web projects, and outlines skills that you need in order to begin a Web project. It then discusses the relationship of technology to the teaching, learning, and evaluation cycle. In this chapter we introduce the concept of *Universal Design for Learning*. The chapter also provides an overview of the qualities of Web projects that make them a powerful and dynamic way to enhance and enrich student learning. And the chapter concludes with descriptions of various Web tools we believe teachers should be familiar with because of the use they receive from students and their potential to provide unique learning opportunities when integrated into the curriculum.

## THE WEB AND DIGITAL NATIVES

It seems oh so long ago when we first heard of a mysterious thing called the World Wide Web. We were fascinated with the concept when we read about it. We were in awe of it when we finally saw a demonstration of what it could do. We were addicted to it once we actually had the opportunity to personally use it. Even though that all now seems so far off, in reality it wasn't that long ago.

The concept of what has become the Web is credited to Tim Berners-Lee while he was a researcher at a physics lab in Switzerland. The issue that Berners-Lee was trying to overcome was the need for physicists to share research documents in an efficient manner with other physicists around the world. His solution was outlined in a proposal he wrote in 1989. His proposed system included three major elements: (1) Hypertext

Markup Language (HTML) to develop documents, (2) Hypertext Transfer Protocol (HTTP) to transmit the created documents, and (3) a software program (a browser) that would receive, interpret, and display data (see Resources for a discussion of these terms). A key concept of the proposal was consistency. Berners-Lee wanted to design a system that would allow users to share and access information no matter what type of computer they were using. A working prototype of this system was not realized until early 1991 when it was used on a single Web server in Switzerland at the physics laboratory (CERN) where Berners-Lee worked. In late 1991, this Web server was made accessible to the general public. By 2002, the number of public Web servers grew to approximately 24 million (Berners-Lee, 1998; Berners-Lee & Feschetti, 2000).

With each passing day, more and more people gain access to the Web. Various studies and surveys indicate that the number of current Web users is anywhere between 500 and 600 million worldwide. This number has increased significantly over the past five years as Internet connectivity has improved and computing hardware and software have continued to become relatively less expensive.

You can almost guarantee that your students will have access to the Web and have some facility using it. For most of you, your students are part of the so-called N-generation or D-generation (net or digital generation). They have grown up during a time when the Web has always been available. Marc Prensky, in his "Digital Natives, Digital Immigrants" (2001), referred to these students as "digital natives." He stated that, "Our students today are all 'native speakers' of the digital language of computers, video games, and the Internet." Prensky believes that these students "think and process information fundamentally differently" than students who grew up in a time without these technologies. Because digital native students are well-versed in the language of the Internet, they will expect, as will their parents, that it is integrated into the classroom.

## WHY USE THE WEB IN THE CLASSROOM?

Despite the expectations placed on teachers to integrate the Web into the curriculum, teachers should not blindly do so without exploring whether it will actually improve student achievement. Teachers should ask: "Why use the Web in the classroom?" When teachers who use the Web in their classrooms are asked this question, some respond, "Because it's fun!" and others claim, "The Web engages students." Some even say, "I use the Web in my class because I like technology." However, for most teachers who are questioning whether to use the Web, the fundamental question is: "Can use of the Web increase student learning?" A second question that teachers often ask is: "Is making use of the Web for in-class activities a professionally responsible thing to do?" As the authors of this book, our answer to both of these questions is an unqualified, "Yes!" Of course a simple yes answer is not enough; we must offer a rationale for why Web-based activities are appropriate and how the Web can make a positive difference in learning.

## Connecting Web Projects to National Standards

Before engaging in the use of the Web in the classroom, teachers have generally asked us one of two questions: "How does the use of technology fit into my curriculum?" and "What do I need to know to be an effective teacher with technology?" We are all aware of the need to make the most of our instructional time. We also understand the importance of connecting what the students do in our classroom to standards. Most states have developed a wide array of curriculum standards. These standards are often a reflection of standards developed by expert groups, including the National Council of Teachers of Mathematics, the National Council of Teachers of English, and the National Academy of Sciences. Utilizing technology is generally woven throughout each set of standards. Most states also recognize a specific set of technology standards developed by the International Society for Technology in Education (ISTE). ISTE has sets of standards for students, teachers, and administrators; the two we will focus on are the ones for students and teachers. The formal names for these are the National Educational Technology Standards for Students (NETS-S) and the National Educational Technology Standards for Teachers (NETS-T). Your school district may have developed an outline of technology skills necessary for each grade level. Most likely this outline is based on the NETS-S. The six NETS-S standards are:

## Technology Foundation Standards for Students[1]

1. Creativity and innovation

   *Students demonstrate creative thinking, construct knowledge, and develop innovative products and processes using technology. Students:*

   a. apply existing knowledge to generate new ideas, products, or processes.

   b. create original works as a means of personal or group expression.

---

1. Reprinted with permission from *National Educational Technology Standards for Students, Second Edition,* © 2007, ISTE (International Society for Technology in Education), iste@iste.org, www.iste.org. All rights reserved. Permission does not constitute an endorsement by ISTE.

    c. use models and simulations to explore complex systems and issues.

    d. identify trends and forecast possibilities.

2. Communication and collaboration

   *Students use digital media and environments to communicate and work collaboratively, including at a distance, to support individual learning and contribute to the learning of others. Students:*

   a. interact, collaborate, and publish with peers, experts, or others employing a variety of digital environments and media.

   b. communicate information and ideas effectively to multiple audiences using a variety of media and formats.

   c. develop cultural understanding and global awareness by engaging with learners of other cultures.

   d. contribute to project teams to produce original works or solve problems.

3. Research and information fluency

   *Students apply digital tools to gather, evaluate, and use information. Students:*

   a. plan strategies to guide inquiry.

   b. locate, organize, analyze, evaluate, synthesize, and ethically use information from a variety of sources and media.

   c. evaluate and select information sources and digital tools based on the appropriateness to specific tasks.

   d. process data and report results.

4. Critical thinking, problem solving, and decision making

   *Students use critical-thinking skills to plan and conduct research, manage projects, solve problems, and make informed decisions using appropriate digital tools and resources. Students:*

   a. identify and define authentic problems and significant questions for investigation.

   b. plan and manage activities to develop a solution or complete a project.

   c. collect and analyze data to identify solutions and/or make informed decisions.

   d. use multiple processes and diverse perspectives to explore alternative solutions.

5. Digital citizenship

   *Students understand human, cultural, and societal issues related to technology and practice legal and ethical behavior. Students:*

   a. advocate and practice safe, legal, and responsible use of information and technology.

     b.  exhibit a positive attitude toward using technology that sup-
        ports collaboration, learning, and productivity.

     c.  demonstrate personal responsibility for lifelong learning.

     d.  exhibit leadership for digital citizenship.

6.  Technology operations and concepts

   *Students demonstrate a sound understanding of technology con-
   cepts, systems, and operations. Students:*

     a.  understand and use technology systems.

     b.  select and use applications effectively and productively.

     c.  troubleshoot systems and applications.

     d.  transfer current knowledge to learning of new technologies.

Teachers, administrators, and parents generally agree that students
need to graduate from our high schools technologically literate. Many educators believe that this requires separate technology classes within schools.
This simply isn't the case. Technology is a tool that is used across content
areas and throughout everyone's daily lives. Technology is not something
that should be considered separate from the curriculum. Instead, our goal
should be to make technology a seamless part of our teaching and instruction. This is a particular challenge to any teacher who does not feel technologically sophisticated or feels less technologically adept than the students.

As teachers, we may question what skills we must have to be effective
in incorporating new technologies (in this case new computing technologies) into our classrooms. There are two ways to address this question. The
first is by identifying teacher competency standards in technology; the
second way is to draw from our own experience. As mentioned previously,
ISTE has a set of standards for the teachers. The NETS-T are as follows:

### Technology Foundation Standards for Teachers[2]

1.  Technology operations and concepts

   *Teachers demonstrate a sound understanding of technology opera-
   tions and concepts. Teachers:*

     a.  demonstrate introductory knowledge, skills, and understand-
        ing of concepts related to technology (as described in the ISTE
        National Education Technology Standards for Students).

---

2. Reprinted with permission from *National Educational Technology Standards for
Students: Connecting Curriculum and Technology.* © 2000, ISTE (International Society for
Technology in Education), iste@iste.org, www.iste.org. All rights reserved. Permission
does not constitute an endorsement by ISTE.

    b. demonstrate continual growth in technology knowledge and skills to stay abreast of current and emerging technologies.

2. Planning and designing learning environments and experiences

   *Teachers plan and design effective learning environments and experiences supported by technology. Teachers:*

       a. design developmentally appropriate learning opportunities that apply technology-enhanced instructional strategies to support the diverse needs of learners.

       b. apply current research on teaching and learning with technology when planning learning environments and experiences.

       c. identify and locate technology resources and evaluate them for accuracy and suitability.

       d. plan for the management of technology resources within the context of learning activities.

       e. plan strategies to manage student learning in a technology-enhanced environment.

3. Teaching, learning, and the curriculum

   *Teachers implement curriculum plans that include methods and strategies for applying technology to maximize student learning. Teachers:*

       a. facilitate technology-enhanced experiences that address content standards and student technology standards.

       b. use technology to support learner-centered strategies that address the diverse needs of students.

       c. apply technology to develop students' higher-order skills and creativity.

       d. manage student learning activities in a technology-enhanced environment.

4. Assessment and evaluation

   *Teachers apply technology to facilitate a variety of effective assessment and evaluation strategies. Teachers:*

       a. apply technology in assessing student learning of subject matter using a variety of assessment techniques.

       b. use technology resources to collect and analyze data, interpret results, and communicate findings to improve instructional practice and maximize student learning.

       c. apply multiple methods of evaluation to determine students' appropriate use of technology resources for learning, communication, and productivity.

5. Productivity and professional practice

   *Teachers use technology to enhance their productivity and professional practice. Teachers:*

   a. use technology resources to engage in ongoing professional development and lifelong learning.
   b. continually evaluate and reflect on professional practice to make informed decisions regarding the use of technology in support of student learning.
   c. apply technology to increase productivity.
   d. use technology to communicate and collaborate with peers, parents, and the larger community in order to nurture student learning.

6. Social, ethical, legal, and human issues

   *Teachers understand the social, ethical, legal, and human issues surrounding the use of technology in PK–12 schools and apply those principles in practice. Teachers:*

   a. model and teach legal and ethical practices related to technology use.
   b. apply technology resources to enable and empower learners with diverse backgrounds, characteristics, and abilities.
   c. identify and use technology resources that affirm diversity.
   d. promote safe and healthy use of technology resources.
   e. facilitate equitable access to technology resources for all students.

Many teachers just starting to integrate technology are intimidated when they read the standards for the first time. Other teachers read the standards and decide that they probably shouldn't use technology because they know so little. This isn't true. If you want to work toward meeting technology standards, you have to start somewhere. The first step should be a small one, one with which you feel comfortable. The next steps should be relatively small as well, allowing yourself to stretch your abilities a bit at a time until one day you find you can apply all the standards with confidence and ease. Approaching new technologies with your students can be a wonderful experience for everyone involved. We have found that students genuinely appreciate the efforts a teacher makes in trying something new that he or she thinks the students will like. Experimenting with a new technology is also a tremendous opportunity to model effective learning and collaboration strategies; of course, our suggestion is to start with a Web project.

Web projects are a sure way to increase your own professional knowledge while having fun in the process. As for minimum skills, if you understand the basics of word processing and how to use a mouse, and have read through this book, you are ready to begin a Web project and include it in your curriculum! Throughout this book we provide specific details on how to design and produce Web pages that will help you in your efforts. We'll also provide ideas for integrating Web-based activities into your curriculum that will help increase student learning.

## Understanding the Teaching and Learning Cycle

The use of the Web can positively enhance and even transform instruction and affect student learning. But does it do so alone? Does the use of the Web magically create learning? Not quite. For Web projects to positively influence learning, they must be implemented within a broader context. This context starts with a deep understanding of the teaching, learning, and evaluation cycle. The use of the Web as a tool throughout this process can create powerful learning opportunities. The teaching and learning cycle is based on this premise: To design effective instruction, we have to understand what it is that our students, based on their age and developmental level, are supposed to know (based on school, district, state, or national standards). We then must understand our students: their strengths, challenges, and individual learning needs. From this we establish goals and objectives. We evaluate the success of the instruction by determining how well the goals and objectives have been met.

The first step a teacher takes in this cycle is to develop a plan for instruction, which includes selecting appropriate methods. Cooperative learning, cooperative inquiry, drill and practice, teacher presentation, and structured discovery are just a few such methods. After a plan is developed, we design a sequence of events and select the media and materials that would be useful. Media includes such things as paper and pencils, visuals (such as overheads, posters, or pictures), sound, video, real-life objects, and, yes, computers and/or other digital technologies. Once we have a plan, we implement our instruction.

During instruction, we actively note what is working and what isn't, and at the end, we assess the students and make two types of judgments: Did the students learn what we hoped they would? And what would we need to do to improve the instruction? When digital technologies are incorporated into this process, learning opportunities can be multiplied. This happens when we take into consideration the practices and ideas presented within a framework called *Universal Design for Learning.*

## Enhancing Learning for All:
## Universal Design for Learning

The concept of Universal Design for Learning (UDL) originated in the field of architecture (architects and engineers now refer to this generally as *universal design*). As designers created buildings that were accessible for individuals with disabilities, buildings became more accessible or "useful" for those without disabilities as well. One example is the use of automatic door openers. Pushing a button or stepping on a mat to open the door makes it possible for a person with a wheelchair to more easily enter and exit a building. Simultaneously, it makes it much easier for a person with full hands (such as at the grocery store) to enter and exit the same building. The design of an automatic door not only benefits the individual with disabilities, it is universally beneficial because it makes *everyone's* life easier.

According to Center for Universal Design at North Carolina State University (Connell, et al., 1997), the basic principles of universal design include:

- The design is useful and marketable to people with diverse abilities.
- The design accommodates a wide range of individual preferences and abilities.
- Use of the design is easy to understand, regardless of the user's experience, knowledge, language skills, or current concentration level.
- The design communicates necessary information effectively to the user, regardless of ambient conditions or the user's sensory abilities.
- The design minimizes hazards and the adverse consequences of accidental or unintended actions.
- The design can be used efficiently and comfortably and with a minimum of fatigue.
- Appropriate size and space is provided for approach, reach, manipulation, and use, regardless of user's body size, posture, or mobility.

UDL applies these same principles to the classroom. Through the use of a wide range of technologies and supportive best practices, we can create classrooms unlike ever before, classrooms designed to enhance learning for a full spectrum of students, from those with learning challenges to those with special gifts and talents. The flexibility of computing tools complements and supports UDL particularly well. Computers can present information by combining sound, text, and images in a variety of ways that support a wide range of users. By applying principles of UDL, students can engage in learning opportunities that have not been possible in traditional classrooms.

According to Meyer and Rose (2002), the three key principles in the UDL framework are:

1. Representing information in multiple formats and media

2. Providing multiple pathways for students' action and expression

3. Providing multiple ways to engage students' interest and motivation

In the following section we share how Web projects fit into the teaching, learning, and evaluation cycle and support the principles of UDL. This sheds light on the question: "What is the fuss all about?"

> ***Curriculum Resource: Web Site.*** For more information on universally designed classrooms, visit the *Center for Applied and Special Technologies* (CAST) Web site at http://www.cast.org. CAST is a not-for-profit organization that uses technology to expand opportunities for all people. This Web site contains multiple links and information to a variety of information and resources. CAST's focus is on the use of digital assistive technologies.

## Interactive Qualities of Digital Media

We can view images and text and hear sound. Each of these media, when made digital, can be used to create highly interactive learning spaces. Digital text can "read itself" aloud; animations can enhance key points; students can navigate through information following their own preferences and at their own pace.

Web projects can present information in a variety of ways, both visually and aurally. Learners can view moving and still images, read text and have text read to them, and have music and sound enhance the effect. Through digital media, students can do such things as participate in virtual travel. They visit foreign places, hear the music and voices of people from other countries, and not only read about the lives of others but have the potential to communicate with real people.

As a student creates Web projects, they not only interact with all kinds of digital media, they interact with other people and ideas. Projects can be varied according to the prior knowledge and skill levels of each student. All students in a classroom can successfully participate in and make a meaningful contribution to a Web project.

## Flexibility for Demonstrating Learning: Multiple Pathways for Expression

As teachers, we often use tests to measure student learning. However, we all know from our own school experience that traditional paper-and-pencil tests do not always show what we know. Web projects lend themselves to performance measures and "authentic assessment." Through Web-based projects, we can create multiple, rich avenues for students to demonstrate learning. Two ways in which the Web can be used for this are through the completion of a project, and through using the Web to create electronic portfolios.

### Curriculum Integration Idea: Individual Web Projects

As mentioned previously, the Web is a natural forum for presenting information through text, video, still images, and sound. These media can be combined in endless ways. Students who engage in a Web project may showcase their individual technology skills, or may use a Web project to show how they met learning objectives. For example, as a culminating project for an English literature class, a student creates a Web site that compares and contrasts several of the works read during the quarter. His Web site may include links to other sites, overviews of important works, and personal insights into concepts or literary elements of each author's major works (see Figure 1.1). This not only shows what levels of understanding the student has gained during the class, but it also creates an artifact of information available for others. Such a project moves well beyond a written essay and becomes much more dynamic, and truly reflective of the learner's understanding.

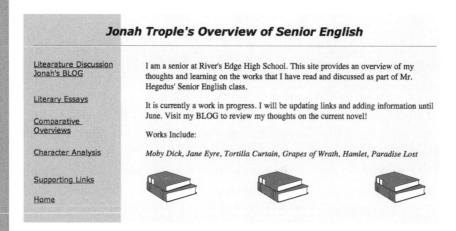

**Figure 1.1**     Sample Individual Student Web Project

*Curriculum Integration Idea: Electronic Portfolios*

Electronic portfolios are a great way for students to compile works that they have completed and display them in an interactive format. Such Web projects can create a rich picture of a student's learning and growth over time. Although advanced e-portfolios are beyond the scope of this book, simple e-portfolios (e.g., a collection of Web pages showcasing a student's writing and/or research) are not difficult to accomplish once you and your students get the hang of making basic Web pages.

For more information on using portfolio assessment see: Hebert, E. A. (2001). *The Power of Portfolios: What Children Can Teach Us About Learning and Assessment.* San Francisco: Jossey-Bass.

## Engaging Students' Interest and Motivation

Today's students are part of the millennial generation and their communication opportunities are vast. Youth of today communicate with friends through cellular phones, e-mail, instant messaging, blogs, and chat rooms. Projects that involve communication through the Web, in the form of a Web site, tap this interest in communication. Students today value technology and want to use technology in the classroom (U.S. Department of Education, 2004). Web projects not only allow students to use digital technologies, which for many is motivation in and of itself, but such projects can often be tailored to individuals, allowing students to engage in projects that are of particular interest to them. For many students, using technology is inherently motivating: it's part of their culture. Engagement is a necessary component in learning. Combine a natural interest and the ability for teachers to differentiate and tailor project requirements and activities, and great chemistry for engaging students can been created.

## Developing Critical-Thinking and Information-Gathering Skills

Research projects in today's classroom are being completely reinvented in our information-rich world. Using encyclopedias, textbooks, and almanacs to answer questions and complete research projects has been replaced with the use of CD-ROMs, DVDs, and the Internet. Sifting through the seemingly endless mass of electronic information requires high levels of critical thinking, especially when we realize that much of the information available through the Web is inaccurate. This has required the creation of new inquiry methods that teach students how to navigate through the "data smog." Such practices develop necessary twenty-first-century critical-thinking and research skills.

---

### Curriculum Integration Idea: WebQuests

WebQuests are online cooperative-grouping research projects. More information can be found at http://webquest.sdsu.edu/. You can even complete a WebQuest about WebQuests that has been designed for teachers by Bernie Dodge by going to http://webquest.sdsu.edu/web questwebquest-hs.html.

---

## Support for Cooperative Work

There is a general myth that if students use technology, they will spend too much time online and will fail to develop social skills outside of cyberspace. This won't happen with a Web project! In the world of technology, teams of people create Web sites and multimedia projects. These teams are dynamic and interactive, and require high levels of engagement. When you begin your Web project with students, you'll see and hear anything but a quiet, individualistic environment. Why? Because Web projects lend themselves to collaborative or cooperative learning.

Cooperative learning is a method of instruction that has a strong research base (Ellis, 2001). Cooperative learning may include the use of partners (peer-mediated instruction) or use larger groups with three to five members. There are many forms of cooperative learning, but in most all models a group is given a specific task and each member of the group is assigned a role or specific activity that will contribute to the completion of the task. Multimedia projects lend themselves to cooperative learning activities. After assigning a Web project, students can be assigned roles that may include such things as:

- *The visual design expert* is responsible for making sure that the Web site follows visual design principles.
- *The image technician* is responsible for finding noncopyrighted images or supplying digital pictures.

- *The content expert* is responsible for adding text to the Web site and reviewing information.
- *The technician* is responsible for troubleshooting or assisting others with the Web editing software.

These are just a few examples as the types of roles are endless. It's up to your imagination and the type of project!

> For more information about setting up and managing multimedia projects, look at *Multimedia Projects in the Classroom: A Guide to Development and Evaluation* by Timothy D. Green and Abbie Brown (2002a).

### How Does the Use of Cooperative Learning Impact Student Achievement?

David Johnson and Roger Johnson (1999), two experts in the field of cooperative learning, identified the valuable outcomes of engaging in cooperative activities.

- *Positive interdependence.* Positive interdependence is when each member of the group needs the other members and each individual has a role that contributes to the overall success of a project. In a group multimedia project, each student role becomes necessary to the success of the project.
- *Face-to-face proximity promotes interaction.* Multimedia projects generally foster interaction. In the field of Web design, groups of people work together and they communicate regularly. In a well-designed cooperative learning project, students will spend much of their time engaged with each other. They will need to communicate to complete a project.
- *Individual and group accountability.* When each person has a role, he or she can be held accountable for completing the assigned task. The group is only successful when the Web project is completed.
- *Interpersonal and small-group skills and group processing.* Students who are working in collaborative teams to complete a Web project will be practicing communication skills and learning how to make group decisions.

## WEB TOOLS TO ENHANCE STUDENT LEARNING

Although the primary focus of this book is on the design, development, and use of Web projects to promote student achievement, there are some unique Web tools that you should be aware of that can be used to enhance student learning. Our goal in providing a list describing these Web tools is to help you understand what is available—it isn't meant to help you learn how to integrate these tools. There are great resources in print (such as *Blogs, Wikis, Podcasts, and Other Powerful Web Tools for Classrooms* by Will Richardson, 2006) and on the Web that can help provide you with guidance on how you might implement these tools in the classroom.

As you read through the list below, keep in mind that it's not exhaustive; however, we believe the list includes the most current and stable Web tools widely used by teachers (and their students!). Also keep in mind that technology changes rapidly and that in the next few years this list could look very different (though we believe many of these tools will be around for years to come).

### Blogs

A blog can be thought of as an online journal. The term *blog* is simply shorthand for *Web log.* Someone who communicates via a blog is known as a *blogger* and the network of blogs is known as the *blogosphere.* Blogs started as online diaries and have rapidly become highly interactive forums for communication. Blogging software allows an individual or a group of individuals to post text, hyperlinks, images, and multimedia. Visitors to a blog can read the postings and search the site (it can be thought of as a highly evolved discussion board). The owner of the blog can add and delete postings and can allow visitors to respond to the postings.

*Curriculum Integration Ideas for Blogs*

Blogging has become much more than the creation of personal diaries; today, blogs are a way to editorialize and promote dialogue on a wide variety of topics. Companies are creating blog software designed specifically for schools and school-age students that is filtered for inappropriate content or can be accessed only by users who have passwords. See http://www.gaggle.com and http://www.schoolblogs.net.

There are numerous unique ways that blogs can be implemented into the curriculum to promote student learning. You only need to use your creativity to determine how it might help meet student learning needs and how blogs could fit into your curriculum. One obvious area is language arts—specifically writing. With access to a blog, students have the opportunity to write and share their work with others. Classmates and others (if appropriate) can then comment on the work their classmates post. This can help build a collaborative learning environment. An added advantage is that students who know that their work will be shared typically take great care in completing their work. Other ideas for the educational use of blogs include using them to:

- Keep a reflective journal.
- Submit assignments for review.
- Work with small groups.
- Create an e-portfolio.
- Manage notes.

Additionally, a teacher's use of a blog can help students! Teachers may use a blog to post instructional notes for students, resources, and annotated links. Teachers can also use blogs to share professional information and ideas with other educators and parents.

## Course Management/Learning Management Systems

Course management and learning management systems (CMS/LMS) are software packages that allow an instructor to deliver portions of or an entire course via a Web-based environment. These software packages attempt to mimic the elements of a traditional face-to-face classroom by providing instructors with the ability to post announcements, give students quizzes and tests, deliver various types of content to students, have students participate and collaborate in asynchronous (not live) and synchronous (live) discussions with fellow students and the instructor, turn in assignments, keep track of student grades, and more.

Various popular CMS/LMS are used in both K–12 and higher education. The systems can be separated into two major categories: commercial and open source. The commercial packages—such as Blackboard, WebCT, and eCollege—are operated and maintained by for-profit companies that charge a license fee to use their system. A school or school district would pay a yearly license fee to have access to the system based on the number of users (students) that would access the system. In return for the license fee, a school or school district would have access to the Web-based system where teachers and students could log in through unique usernames and passwords. Open-source CMS/LMS are created by individuals or organizations that are not-for-profit. The idea behind open-source software is that anyone can use the software and make changes to it, as long as the changes are shared with the public. Two of the most popular open-source CMS/LMS are Moodle and Sakai. A license fee is not required to use either one; however, they do not come with the support that a commercial CMS/LMS provides. If a school district uses Moodle or Sakai, the support will need to come from the school district's technical support.

---

### Curriculum Integration Ideas for CMS/LMS

With either a commercial or open-source CMS/LMS, a teacher would be provided with a unique "classroom" space that only his or her students could access. The teacher could use the classroom space as he or she felt necessary to either supplement or replace what took place in the classroom. A typical scenario we have observed for using a CMS/LMS in the K–12 classroom is to use the space to place extra credit assignments for students to complete that will help extend what students have learned during normal classroom time. A teacher might place content for students to read, listen to, and view (or all three) and then have students complete an activity that is explained online in the classroom space. Another example is to deliver an entire course through the use of a CMS/LMS. We have worked with high schools that have delivered various courses through this type of system. There are even virtual high schools that deliver their entire curriculum through a Web-based learning environment that uses a course management or learning management system. The gifted and talented high school run by Stanford University is a recent example of this.

---

The advantage of using a CMS/LMS is the ability to deliver content to students and have them participate in activities whenever they have the time and a connection to the Internet. Numerous benefits can be realized from using a course management or learning management system:

1. Students who miss time at school for various reasons can access assignments missed due to their absence.

2. Content and learning activities can be extended beyond the class-room for gifted students.

3. Courses can be delivered to student populations that may not have access to these courses; for example, middle school students in a rural location can be offered a foreign language course that isn't available through their school district.

Disadvantages of using such as system include:

1. Costs can be prohibitive, such as license fees for using a commer-cial version or the maintenance costs of keeping an open-source version running.

2. It places a burden on a teacher to use and maintain a course Web space; this takes time that generally is not supported during the regular school workday.

3. As with all Web tools, access for students is an issue; not all students will have access to the Internet outside of school.

Despite the disadvantages, CMS/LMS do provide unique learning opportunities. Their use in higher education has grown significantly in the past five years, and the use in K–12 is steadily increasing as well.

## Instant Messaging

Instant messaging (IM) is a tool that allows you to carry on a synchro-nous (live) conversation with another individual or individuals. The con-versations that take place through IM are typically text based and are carried out through the Web. Various IM software is available, such as Yahoo! Messenger, AOL Instant Messenger, ICQ, and MSN Messenger. Typically, these are available as free downloads, if you sign up for an account with the organization providing the IM tool (for example, you would need to sign up with Yahoo! for a free e-mail account in order to use their IM tool; your e-mail account name would then become your IM user-name). Handheld devices such as cell phones and personal digital assis-tants (like Palm Pilots) can also be used to send instant messages, if they have access to the Internet.

The way an IM tool works is rather straightforward. Let's imagine that you have gone to Yahoo! and signed up for a free e-mail account. You now have a username you can use with their IM tool. Once you have downloaded Yahoo! Messenger, you can send messages to others who also have Yahoo! Messenger on their computer and have a Yahoo!

username (this is important to keep in mind; generally, you can only IM with others who have the same IM tool as you do). When you open Yahoo! Messenger on your computer, you type in the username of the person you want to talk with and a message. If that person is online and has Yahoo! Messenger opened, he or she will receive your message. Typically, users will be alerted (via a dialogue box or sound) that they have a message waiting. After reading the message, he or she can respond to your message by typing in text and pressing the send button. The message will then be sent back to you. A conversation is now taking place!

The major advantage of IM is its synchronous nature. Individuals can carry on a conversation as if they were present in the same room. The exchange of ideas can take place quickly. Granted, various elements of a face-to-face conversation are lost—such as body language and eye contact.

---

### Curriculum Integration Ideas for Instant Messaging

IM has become an integral part of the digital generation's social structure; most students are already using this technology to communicate with their friends while they are simultaneously performing a variety of other tasks on the computer. However, with some direction, students can be taught how to use IM to complete school projects, especially group-oriented tasks. For example, during an environmental studies unit, a science teacher may assign a group of students the task of locating and comparing and contrasting various global projects that promote sustainable living. Students from the same group can use IM to share information and communicate as each individual uses the Web to complete his or her portion of the group task.

---

Using IM in the curriculum can provide students with the opportunity to go beyond the classroom and the normal classroom day. Students can IM with students from their own class about content and assignments for clarification and assistance. This can be done while students are at home working on assignments and projects. Students could IM with students and others throughout the United States, and even the world. IM can provide unique opportunities for students to connect and collaborate. As with any form of communication and collaboration, caution needs to be taken. Students should be made aware of the dangers of talking with individuals they do not personally know. Students should also be given ground rules as to when IM is and is not appropriate.

## Podcasts

A podcast is an audio or video file created and placed on the Web for individuals to download and listen to on their computers or digital media players. Digital media players are handheld devices that store and play audio and video files. The Apple iPod is probably the most popular example of a digital media player (which is where the term *podcast* comes from).

Podcasting works similarly to a subscription service. Once you choose a podcast that you'd like to receive (for example, NBC's *Meet the Press,* or the *Science at NASA Feature Stories* podcasts) you subscribe to that podcast, which means you set your computer—through a program such as Apple's iTunes—to look for and receive those audio or video files, and to update your MP3 player with copies of the most recent files. You can view received podcasts on your computer or on a digital media player. *Podcasting* is the generally accepted term for both audio and video files, but video file distribution is sometimes referred to as *vodcasting.*

Podcast files are available on a variety of Web sites. Sites like The Podcast Directory (http://www.podcast.net/) can help you locate podcasts of interest to you. One of the most popular and extensive podcast collections is located at Apple's iTunes Music Store. Accessing the store requires the use of iTunes software (which is free and runs on both Mac and PC platforms).

Podcasting is seen by many as a potentially powerful instructional medium. Podcasts can be made and distributed via the Web by a variety of people, ranging from big-budget producers to individuals with almost no budget. It is relatively easy and very inexpensive to set up audio and video podcasting. This means podcasting may be a useful educational tool for two very different activities: receiving content from experts, and as a means of student media production.

---

*Curriculum Integration Idea: Podcasts*

Probably the most common and current use of podcasts in education is for summarizing course content and providing extra information to students. Podcasts are a great way to summarize lecture notes or provide additional information on a topic for students to listen to on either a computer or a portable MP3 device. Students have the advantage of being able to listen to material multiple times if they could not comprehend it the first time they encountered the material. This use is also good for English language learners. They are may stop, rewind, and play the content as many times as is necessary. In addition, teachers can work with students to develop podcasts that help them demonstrate understanding of content. A podcast could be used in place of a written essay.

### RSS

RSS stands for *real simple syndication* or *rich site summary*. This Web tool allows you to gather information from certain Web sites and display this information on your own site. Let's explain how this can happen. Certain Web sites contain content that is generated and displayed using code called XML (extensible mark-up language; a cousin to HTML, which you will read about later in this book). The content that is created by the XML code (referred to as a *feed* like a "news feed") can be subscribed to so that you don't have to continue to physically visit the site to get the content. In essence, the content comes to you rather than you having to go out and get it. This is done through another software tool called an aggregator or feed collector. When you want to view the content that has been gathered, you would open the aggregator. The aggregator would gather the new content from the sites with RSS feeds to which you subscribed. You could then read and organize the content.

---

*Curriculum Integration Idea: RSS*

How could a teacher take advantage of RSS? One simple way to take advantage of this tool is to use it to collect information from sites you visit often and then share the information with your students. As a social studies teacher who focuses on U.S. government, you could subscribe to a number of sites that provide current events information about what is taking place within the U.S. government. You would find your favorite Web sites that have RSS feeds and subscribe to the sites (many news organizations and periodicals make RSS feeds available). You would then subscribe to each site only once. After subscribing to a site, every time you open your aggregator you could read the new content that site has provided.

Now that you have done this, what could you do with the information? The following are three possible options out of many: You could make the information available to your students on your own Web site; this information could be part of extra credit or required reading. You could use the information to inform your own teaching by providing you with informational resources. Finally, you could print off the information and share with your students for use in the curriculum. The information could be used as research sources for your students as they explore various topics within the curriculum.

Various Web sites (see the "Going Beyond the Chapter" section of this chapter) explore the process of subscribing to a Web site that makes RSS feeds available, using an aggregator to gather and manipulate the information, and displaying this information on your own Web site. You will discover that RSS has great potential of providing teachers and students with a wealth of current information about various topics that are covered in the curriculum.

## Social Spaces

A number of Web sites exist for the purpose of allowing people to learn more about and communicate with other people. These are known as social networks or social spaces. A popular example of a social space Web site is MySpace (http://www.myspace.com). On a social space Web site, you can set up an individual account (you create an account name and password that allows you to update and make changes); you then post information about yourself as part of a personal profile that is accessible to the larger network. How much information you provide about yourself is up to you. Some social spaces limit the amount of information you can provide (for example, some social spaces do not allow individuals to post telephone numbers or last names). The information you post in your profile becomes part of a large database that other members of the network can search through.

Members of a social space may search for other members who share similar interests and are located near them. A social space also allows people from very different geographic locations to communicate easily. Most social spaces have messaging software built into them, allowing users to send and receive messages to one another on the site itself. Members may also become part of special interest groups within the larger social space.

Social spaces have been under a great deal of scrutiny recently because of the dangers associated with presenting personal information in a public space and because of the threat of predators. Posting too much information can have serious repercussions; for example, an article in *eSchool News* ("Warnings About Social-Networking Sites," 2006) reports that a college freshman's joke about assassinating the president, posted in his social space profile, led to a visit from the Secret Service. Predators have also used social spaces to take advantage of minors. An article in *Time* magazine (Rawe, 2006) reports that a great many young people have received sexual solicitations online. A danger of social space communication is that individuals may not be who they say they are: a teenager could present himself as a college student; a middle-aged adult could easily present herself as a teenager. Because of the dangers associated with social spaces, we suggest being cautious with how you integrate these into the curriculum. Our caution has led us not to include curriculum integration ideas for social spaces.

## Wikis

A wiki (pronounced wee-kee) is a Web page or site that can be modified by anyone who visits the site. Wikis are like traditional Web sites because they have a URL and they can contain text, images, hyperlinks, and multimedia. They are unlike traditional Web sites in that they are dynamic, meaning they are easily manipulated by others and not just the owner of the Web site. A well-known wiki is Wikipedia (http://www .wikipedia.com/), an online encyclopedia where contributors continually update and add to the entries. A wiki user does not have to have specialized Web-editing software installed on his or her computer to edit the wiki. The editing feature is available through the Web site. This enables multiple users to make changes to the site rather easily. It's important to note that because wikis are very easy to contribute to and are not often closely controlled by an individual or group, *anyone* may add to and update entries on all topics. This creates an environment where erroneous or misleading information about a topic may be posted.

---

*Curriculum Integration Idea: Wikis*

Wikis are being used as collaborative spaces where people share their work, as online journals, as discussion sites, and even as a means to archive an individual's work. You can see a comparison of wiki software by going to the Wikipedia at: http://en.wikipedia.org/wiki/ Comparison_of_wiki_software. Like blogs, wikis have the ability to provide students with a collaborative forum where they can write and share information. A wiki could be integrated as a learning tool into various curriculum areas where the goal is for students to share their knowledge in a collaborative manner. For example, students in a history course could use a wiki to write a group report on a historical event. The wiki could be accessed by each group member. The final project would be online and could be shared not only with the teacher but with other students in the history class. In future history classes, the teacher could use the reports saved in the wiki as starting-off points for other groups to add to or create reports (wiki entries) on related historical events.

Although the seven tools we have described allow you to use the Web in unique ways by creating and sharing information, be aware that you are not designing and developing a Web page or site by using these tools. You are using tools that are designed primarily for communicating through the Web via different methods. These tools do have the potential to affect student learning in unique ways.

## SUMMARY

This chapter provided an overview of the National Education Technology Standards for students and for teachers, and provided an explanation of the importance of including Web projects as part of your curriculum. An overview of the teaching and learning cycle was discussed, as were the principles of UDL, which makes it possible to create classrooms where all students are successful. The qualities that help Web projects affect student learning were identified and described. These qualities include: interactive qualities of digital media: a variety of formats and media; and flexibility for demonstrating learning: multiple pathways for expression, engaging students' interest and motivation, developing critical-thinking and information-gathering skills, and support for cooperative learning. The chapter also included descriptions of various Web tools that can be integrated into the classroom. These included blogs, CMS/LMS, IM podcasts, RSS, social networking, and wikis.

The undertaking of a Web project has the potential to change your classroom. Including technology within the teaching and learning cycle, while applying the principles of UDL, creates a highly differentiated, highly interactive, and engaging learning space. With this book and time to practice, you will be ready to embark on your own technological transformation, which will help enhance your students' achievement.

## GOING BEYOND THE CHAPTER

1. **Visit the ISTE Web site.**

   You will find more information about the NETS-T and NETS-S and view technology-infused lesson plan ideas by visiting http://cnets.iste.org/. Most states have adopted either the ISTE technology standards or have developed their own. We suggest that you conduct a search to find out if your state has adopted its own standards.

2. **Universal Design for Learning.**

   See tutorials and examples of UDL in action at http://www .cast.org/teachingeverystudent/.

3. **Other Web Tools.**

   You can read more about the various Web tools we described in this chapter. You can even experiment with using these tools to determine how they might fit within your curriculum. We suggest these sites to begin your exploration.

   - News article on blogging in a school in the U.K.: http://news. bbc.co.uk/1/hi/magazine/3804773.stm
   - Blogs created by elementary students in the United States: http://itc.blogs.com/alejandra/
   - An article from *EDUCAUSE Quarterly* on the benefits and disadvantages of Wikis: http://www.educause.edu/pub/ er/erm04/erm0452.asp?bhcp=1
   - Wiki space for teachers: http://www.wikispaces.com/ site/for/teachers
   - A discussion of RSS for Educators (a PDF document): http://www.weblogg-ed.com/wp-content/uploads/2006/ 05/RSSFAQ4.pdf
   - A list of educational podcasts to get an idea of what is available and how they work: http://epnweb.org/
   - Another listing of educational podcasts; this site also describes simple steps on how to create a podcast by clicking on "Cast" link: http://www.cobb.k12.ga.us/instructional technology/mac/PC/PCGaETC.htm

- RSS: Another site on RSS use for teachers. This is a link to a presentation that was made on the topic: http://www .thinkfree.com/common/view.tfo?method=viewPublish &uid=27750&fno=309490

# Using and Evaluating Web Activities and Projects in the Classroom

## GUIDING QUESTIONS

This chapter will help you answer the following questions:

- How can students use the Web as a research tool?
- How can the Web be integrated into cooperative learning-based activities?
- How can the Web be used for problem-based learning?
- What are some examples of teachers and students making use of the Web for teaching and learning?
- How can the Web be used to help students meet content and technology standards?
- How can I teach my students to effectively evaluate the information they find on Web sites?
- What elements are important to evaluate with student-created Web-based projects?
- What process should I use to evaluate Web-based projects my students create?

## KEY TERMS

| | |
|---|---|
| Content | Search Engine |
| Multimedia | Search Index |
| Problem-Based Learning | Spinning the Web |
| Process | Surfing the Web |
| Product | Threaded Discussions |
| Reliability | Validity |

## OVERVIEW

As discussed in Chapter 1, the Web has been available to the general public for less than fifteen years. Yet, in that short time it has dramatically changed the public perception of what it means to access information, to communicate, and to conduct research. References to the Web are everywhere: on television; in magazines; in motion pictures; the term *dot-com* has become a fixture in the English language. For teachers, this means that Web-based classroom activities have become an expectation. Parents, administrators, and students expect teachers to allow and encourage use of the Web in the classroom. The question every teacher currently faces is: "How do I make good use of this powerful 'thing' in helping my students learn content and meet standards?" This chapter presents ideas for incorporating the Web into classroom activities as both a research tool and a production medium, with the goal of helping your students learn content and skills that will assist them in meeting state and national standards. This chapter also explores the concept of evaluation and how it fits with the use of Web projects in the classroom.

### What Is the Web Again?

Let's take a step back and review. What is the Web, again? As mentioned in Chapter 1, the Web is an Internet-based communication medium. The Internet is the network of all computers connected together around the world using *TCP/IP* (Transmission Control Protocol/Internet Protocol). TCP/IP is the agreed-upon standard by which information is sent through the Internet from one computer to another. The Web uses an additional standard called *HTTP* (Hypertext Transfer Protocol). HTTP allows Web-based content, programmed using *HTML* (Hypertext Markup Language), to be sent from one computer to another through the Internet. The most common method of viewing Web content is to use *browser software* (two of the most popular browsers are Microsoft Internet Explorer and Netscape Navigator). Browser software acts as a translator that takes HTML and formats it so it can be displayed on a computer screen.

Content on the Web is divided into individual computer files called *pages.* A collection of pages closely related to each other, usually created and managed by one person or group, is referred to as a *site.* For example, the *New York Times* puts its content on the Web; the entire collection of content administered by the *New York Times* is its Web site; each individual news story is a page (a discrete file) on the site.

The Web can be used to receive information generated by others, making it a research tool. The Web can also be used to broadcast information for others to receive. The San Diego Zoo, the Metropolitan Museum of Art, and the City of Chicago all have Web sites that offer information about their organization and constituency. A common term for viewing Web-based information (most often by viewing a number of different Web sites) is *surfing.*

The Web is, for the most part, a public space. No governing body restricts or approves of the information made available via the Web. National and regional copyright laws apply to the Web, meaning that it's almost always a crime to place the intellectual property of another person on the Web without his or her permission, but there are no restrictions on what one may make available on the Web if it is one's own property. This means that anyone with server space (this is explained more completely in Chapter 3) can create a Web site that everyone connected to the Internet may view. Web files can also be created for personal or small-group use by distributing the files without posting them to the Web. Making Web pages, or more precisely creating HTML files, is often referred to as *spinning* Web pages.

## INTEGRATING THE WEB INTO THE CURRICULUM: SURFING THE WEB (RESEARCH)

One fantastic feature of the Web is that it can provide a wide variety of information in various media formats. One can find reams of text on just about any subject, as well as multimedia archives and live camera feeds from around the world. For this reason, educators often point out that the Web is particularly useful as a resource for students conducting research. Surfing the Web can also serve as a brainstorming activity for students, giving them an overview on a subject and how that subject is addressed in popular media and by various interest groups. Used well, the Web can serve as a starting point for more detailed examination of a subject, pointing students toward other resources found in the home, school, and library.

> ***Classroom Resource: Web Site.*** A site like Wikipedia (http://www.wikipedia.com/) can be a great place for students to start gathering information on a variety of topics. This site is an online encyclopedia of almost any topic you can imagine. Even though it's full of interesting and useful information, it's important to keep in mind that not all information on the Web can or should be trusted as accurate (more on this idea later in the chapter).

## Using the Web to Send and Receive Messages

Sources of information on the Web often include an e-mail address to which students may send questions and comments. Some Web sites are also set up to allow for an ongoing discussion of sorts; a series of messages are posted directly to the Web site (called a *threaded discussion*), and students may participate in these. Direct access to people outside the classroom can lead to discussion about primary and secondary sources of information. In addition, some Web sites are set up as blogs (see Chapter 1) that allow individuals to post comments about information they find on the site. This is similar to a threaded discussion.

*Classroom Integration Idea: Examples of Blogs by Students and Teachers*

> http://weblogs.hcrhs.k12.nj.us/bees/
>
> http://www.polar06.yesican-projects.ca/Blog/
>
> http://teachersteachingteachers.org/
>
> http://classblogmeister.com/blog.php?blogger_id=59644
>
> http://itc.blogs.com/thewriteweblog/

*Curriculum Integration Idea: Telementors*

The ability to bring other voices into the classroom, especially those with expertise in the discipline students are researching, makes the Web and the Internet a powerful supplemental tool in the classroom. More traditional methods of long-distance communication (the telephone, the postal service) are often too costly or take too much time. One activity that matches students through e-mail and the Web with experts is called *telementoring*. Bare and Meek (1998) indicated that the purpose of tele-mentoring programs has been to match K–12 students with experienced experts and professionals in order to provide students with real-world insights into the curriculum they are studying. When students connect with professionals, the enthusiasm students display toward the research project increases, as does the quality of the work students produce.

Using telementoring in your classroom can be accomplished in various ways. Three common approaches to telementoring are:

1. mentors who act as experts agreeing to respond to questions sent through e-mail or posted on a Web site; this is often the most typical type of telementoring;

2. a mentor paired with a student; this type of telementoring scenario is rare; an example of this scenario is a graduate student who provides assistance to a student completing a research paper on a topic in the graduate student's area of study; and

3. mentors who are involved in a partnership arrangement; often this telementoring scenario involves large corporations that have employees who agree to act as mentors in a particular discipline (such as science, computer science, or math) for a school or school district for a period of time.

Telementoring can provide your students with tremendous opportunities to have firsthand discussions with experts. Students can conduct research using primary sources. If you are interested in including this type of activity into your classroom, we suggest you visit http://www.telementoring.org/ to learn more about the topic and to read what type of opportunities exist for your classroom and curriculum.

---

*Curriculum Integration Idea: Ask an Expert*

In addition to telementoring, another great way for your students to access experts in various areas is at http://www.askanexpert.com/. There are numerous categories—such as animals, health, and art/humanities—on which students can send a question to an expert in this area. Typically, students will need to include an e-mail address along with their name when submitting a question. The site also includes links to Web sites of various experts, which can allow students to conduct a preliminary search for their answer prior to sending the question to the expert.

## Safety and Netiquette

The Web is an open environment, and like any open environment it has its positive and negative aspects. Just as young people are taught the conventions of crossing streets carefully and dealing with strangers in order to avoid problems on the main street in any town, they must be taught the general rules of etiquette and safety that allow them to avoid problems while using the Internet and Web. This topic is covered in more detail in Chapter 4; however, it is worth introducing here.

You and your students should adhere to two major safety rules.

1. Never give out identifying information to strangers (this includes posting information by filling out forms). If the class is creating a Web site, do not combine students' names with their pictures.

2. Do not believe everything you see and read. Keep in mind that a person may be "presenting" as something he or she is not. (A 50-year-old woman may use the screen name "coolguy12" but it doesn't mean she is a guy, 12 years old, or even cool).

In general, the same rules that apply to any correspondence apply to the Internet. The term *netiquette* has been given to the etiquette guidelines one should use when communicating online. These guidelines are especially important if you have your students participate in activities such as telementoring, in which students are working with individuals who are sharing their time and expertise. Shea (1994) provided ten such guidelines for communicating online.

1. Remember the human.

2. Adhere to the same standards of behavior online that you follow in real life.

3. Know where you are in cyberspace.

4. Respect other people's time and bandwidth.

5. Make yourself look good online.

6. Share expert knowledge.

7. Help keep flames under control.

8. Respect other people's privacy.

9. Don't abuse your power.

10. Be forgiving of other people's mistakes.

## Searching the Web: Engines and Indexes

Using the Web for research requires that students have the skills and knowledge they need to find relevant information on the topic they are researching. Students should be familiar with the two types of search tools that exist to assist people in locating resources on the Web: indexes and search engines. An index attempts to systematically arrange Web sites and pages, putting them in an alphabetical, chronological, geographical, or subject-oriented order. Locating information using an index is performed by following category headings to a listing of specific Web sites. For example looking for Web sites related to antique collecting may require following the subject heading "Entertainment," to the subheading "Hobbies," to the next subheading "Collectibles," and so on. Indexes require a great deal of human effort in terms of collecting, arranging, coding, and annotating information (Liu, 1996). One of the best known examples of a Web index is Yahoo! (http://www.yahoo.com/), an extensive listing of Web sites and resources organized by subject. Yahoo! has a "kid-friendly" version of its Web index called Yahoo! Kids (http://kids.yahoo.com).

Unlike an index, a search engine collects Web resources automatically. Instead of browsing or accepting submissions of Web sites and pages, search engines use software programs that automatically search through the Web, using keywords and Boolean terms (*and, or,* and *not* are Boolean terms). The programs collect information about public Web files, then sort the information gathered into a searchable database. Search engines have two components: collection and search. The software responsible for collection roams the Internet, gathering information about Web sites, which it then sorts and indexes, creating a searchable database. This database can be sifted through using the search engine's second component, the search interface (Liu, 1996). Currently, one of the most popular search engines is Google (http://www.google.com/).

Several factors determine the usefulness of both search engines and indexes. Size, content, currency of the database, search speed, and the interface design are considered critically important in deciding how well search engines and indexes work. Most popular search sites like Yahoo! and Google make use of a combination of search engines and indexes; at the very least these sites link to each other to make searching easier if their site cannot provide the information requested.

Making use of a variety of search engines and indexes, and evaluating their effectiveness can provide students with an excellent introduction to the essential elements of library science. The organization of information is one of the most basic elements of good scholarship, and the fact that a wide variety of search tools can be accessed easily on the Web makes it an excellent classroom resource.

## Evaluating Web Sites

Although the Web can be an excellent classroom resource for students as they conduct research, we've found that many of our students believe that if information is found on a Web site, the information must be true. To some degree, we can't fault our students because many bogus Web sites exist that seem quite believable and authoritative. Many adults are even fooled by some of these sites! One great example of a site that seems very believable and authoritative, but is completely bogus, is one about the Pacific Northwest Tree Octopus (http://zapatopi .net/treeoctopus.html). We encourage you to visit this site to see for yourself how believable such a site can be when it is well designed and thought out.

Sites like the Pacific Northwest Tree Octopus are intended as jokes and can be quite entertaining. Other sites, however, put forth inaccurate information in an attempt to sway impressionable minds. Sites that offer "proof" of the validity of intolerant behavior such as racism or religious persecution are dangerous because they seem to be presenting scientific information when in fact they are nothing more than the personal opinion of an individual or group.

Because sites like this exist on the Web, we feel it's important that our students have the skills that allow them to successfully discriminate the information they find on the Web sites they visit. With this in mind, we believe you must directly teach your students skills on how to critically evaluate the Web sites they view, and provide them with opportunities to practice critical evaluation skills. They need to be able to determine if the information they read is both valid and reliable. The International Society for Technology Educators (ISTE) supports this idea. In ISTE's National Educational Technology Standards (NETS) for Students, Standard 5—Technology Research Tools—reads in part, "Students use technology to locate, evaluate, and collect information from a variety of sources" (Kelly, 2002). The American Library Association also deals with this idea in Standard 2 of their Information Literacy Standards, which reads, "The student who is information literate evaluates information critically and competently" (American Library Association, 2005). The idea of critically evaluating information is also supported throughout various content standards.

## What Is Validity and Reliability?

Scientists and scholars speak of the validity and reliability of research protocols. A valid study addresses the issues in question. A researcher will ask, "Did this study actually measure what it said it wanted to measure?" A reliable one allows for reproducible experiments. The question asked here is, "Can this study be repeated and still have the same outcome?" Validity and reliability of information are issues that even the youngest researchers must address.

Two traditional methods of gathering and distributing information are through the disciplines of journalism and academic scholarship. Journalism is the art of conducting research and presenting its results through media that is available to the general public. Newspapers, magazines, television, and radio broadcasts are traditional media for journalists, and many journalistic organizations now have Web sites of their own (e.g., NYTimes.com, CNN.com). Journalists do their best to verify that their sources are accurate; they submit their stories to editors who decide whether the story is both truthful and something the public will be interested in seeing.

Academic scholarship is part of conducting research and presenting its results for groups of people who have specific interests and areas of expertise. Academics traditionally perform their experiments at universities and other research institutions; they share the results of their research by publishing them in special interest journals or presenting their results at conferences. Work that is submitted for inclusion in a journal or conference is often reviewed by other members of the same field; this is called *jury* or *peer* review. The intention of this type of review is to make sure that whatever is presented is valid and of significant interest to other specialists in that area.

In both journalism and academic scholarship, some organizations are more trusted for reliability and accuracy than are others. *The New York Times*, for example, is considered by many people to be the United States' news source of record (that is, quoting *The New York Times* is almost always a reflection of the accuracy of a statement).

The Web provides a great deal of information, but determining the validity and reliability of the information can be difficult. We would like to suggest that this difficulty is exactly why the Web makes an excellent learning tool for young researchers. It gives teachers and students an opportunity to discuss the issues of information validity and reliability using what Reigeluth (1983) called "divergent examples"—instances in which it may be difficult to decide whether the example fits the definition of the idea or concept under discussion.

## Teaching Students to Critically Evaluate Web Sites: Is the Information Valid and Reliable?

Because Web content is not controlled, the information the Web provides runs the full range: famous scholars may post the results of carefully conducted research; creative artists may post completely original works; and would-be experts may post completely bogus information that has the look and feel of art or scholarship. And yes, there's a large amount of "adult-oriented" content that one must contend with. With the exception of the adult-oriented sites, this wide variety of information may be one of the Web's biggest advantages as a teaching tool. However, the fact that the Web is an open environment where all kinds of information, real and imagined, are made available solidifies the point that students must have the skills to determine what information presented is valid and reliable.

***Our Approach.*** Our approach to helping students critically analyze Web content focuses on a series of questions that your students should be able to answer about a Web site. The younger your students are, the more guidance they will need answering the questions; you may even need to modify the questions. As you teach your students how to evaluate Web sites, we suggest walking them through the evaluation process several times before letting them loose to do it on their own. We also suggest coming back to this idea periodically throughout the school year.

We divide the questions into two areas: purpose and content. We have our students start out by looking at the purpose of the Web site and then move into analyzing the content. The questions we have them answer are provided below.

***Purpose.*** What is the purpose of the Web site? Every Web site has a purpose, but it isn't always obvious. If it isn't obvious what the purpose of the site is, your students should immediately be skeptical of the information they find there. There are elements to look for in trying to evaluate a Web site's purpose. Have your students look at each of these areas to formulate the site's purpose.

- *The URL or Web address.* Knowing what kind of organization the Web site is originating from provides clues as to its purpose. Therefore, have your students take a look at the domain name of the Web address as they begin to analyze the purpose of the Web site. The following are a few of the most common domain names and what they are intended to indicate.
  o .edu—an educational institution
  o .com—a for-profit business
  o .org—a nonprofit organization
  o .gov—the U.S. government
  o .mil—the U.S. military
      In addition, there are also country domain names. For example, .mx stands for Mexico. The official site for the Mexican government reads—http://www.presidencia.gob.mx/
- *The titles and headings.* The titles and headings of a Web site can provide information that helps determine what that site's purpose is. It's much like reading the titles and headings in a book to get a glimpse into what you are about to read.
- *The images.* Have your students examine the images for possible clues about the purpose of the site. Images on a site can provide insight into the site's purpose. If there are advertisements on a site, your students should know that the information they read may be biased.

While examining these elements, your students should ask:

- Who is the intended audience for this information?
- What is the information presented intending to convey?
- Why has this person or organization chosen to present this information on the Web?
- What clues do the domain name, heading/titles, and images provide as to the purpose of the site?

**Content.** Although a Web site may have a wonderful purpose, there might be issues with the content. The content could very well not match or help meet the purpose of the Web site. We feel that several areas are helpful to focus on when examining the content provided on a Web site. Have your students examine the following areas and provide answers to the questions in the list below.

Your students may find it difficult to answer these questions with some sites. It's still important, however, to have them try. They need to establish the habit of critically evaluating every site they visit, because the more information they have about a Web site, the less likely they will believe inaccurate or biased information.

- Authority
  - What information is provided about the person or organization presenting the information?
  - Can it be clearly determined who is responsible for the Web site?
  - Is the person or organization considered to be expert in the area being presented on the Web site?
- Scope
  - Is there any depth of detail provided, or is the content just presented in a superficial way?
- Accuracy
  - Is there any blatantly inaccurate information?
  - Is there a bibliography or works cited section within the site?
  - Is it free of grammar and spelling errors?
- Bias
  - Is the information presented in a fair and objective manner?
  - Is there a company sponsoring the Web page, and if so, what self-interest may it have in supporting the site?
  - Why is the person or organization providing this information interested in doing so?
- Currency
  - Is there a date indicating when the site was last updated?

*Curriculum Resource: Rubric—Web Site Content Critique Form*

Figure 2.1 contains an example of a Web site critique form that we use with our students as we teach them how to critically analyze a Web site and the content they are reading.

| **Web Address:** | |
|---|---|
| *Purpose* | |
| What do you believe is the purpose of the Web site?<br><br>What clues do you have that helped you make your conclusion? | |
| *Content* | |
| 1. What information is provided about the person or organization presenting the information? | |
| 2. Can it be clearly determined who is responsible for the Web site? | |
| 3. Is the person or organization considered to be expert in the area being presented on the Web site? | |
| 4. Is there any depth of detail provided, or is the content just presented in a superficial way? | |
| 5. Is there any blatantly inaccurate information? | |
| 6. Is there a bibliography or works cited section within the site? | |
| 7. Is it free of grammar and spelling errors? | |
| 8. Is the information presented in a fair and objective manner? | |
| 9. Is there a company sponsoring the Web page, and if so, what self-interest may it have in supporting the site? | |
| 10. Why is the person or organization providing this information interested in doing so? | |
| 11. Is there a date that shows when the site was last updated? | |
| What is your overall assessment of the Web site's content? | |

**Figure 2.1**     Web Site Evaluation Form

*Additional Methods for Evaluating Web Sites*

In addition to the framework we have provided, various other approaches exist. A basic Web search conducted using online search tools like Google or Yahoo! (using the terms *evaluating Web sites*) will provide you with various links to sites that provide different approaches. After using our approach with your students to get them comfortable with the process, we suggest looking at a few different approaches in order for you to create a process specifically tailored for your students.

## Examples of Using the Web for Research in the Classroom

We have all become familiar with the phrase, "surfing the Internet." The word *surf* implies riding a wave; the rider follows the surge and direction the wave prescribes. The Web has forever transformed how we conduct research; therefore, our students must do more than merely surf. Our students must learn how to avoid becoming lost in the endless sea of information and shipwrecking on the shore of misinformation. Historically, student research projects have focused on finding information. Today, we focus on helping students learn to *ask* and *answer* good questions with accurate information. Teachers and students must plan for purposeful investigations.

Traditionally teachers have assigned research topics for their students. For example, in fifth grade a teacher may ask a student to "find out about Rhode Island." These types of reports have helped students learn to gather information from such sources as books, pamphlets, almanacs, and encyclopedias. A student gathered all of the books in school on a particular state (or topic) and summarized the pertinent information. During the process the student was relatively sure that the information gathered was accurate. With the Internet, it's not possible to read through all of the available information, and it's often difficult to determine what information is reliable.

Many models of Web-based research projects can help students learn to use a research process. Big6 (http://www.big6.com/) is an information literacy model that can be used for both Web-based and traditional research projects. Jaimie McKenzie's research cycle (1995) is similar to Big6, but focuses on the use of the Web.

According to the Jaimie McKenzie research cycle, there are seven stages in the research process: questioning, planning, gathering, sorting and sifting, synthesizing, evaluating, and reporting. Fundamental to this process is the development of an essential question. This is more than simply stating, "find out about _____." Instead, it is articulating a question that stimulates higher-level thinking. Below are two examples (one from an elementary classroom and the other from a secondary classroom) that follow this process that effectively uses the Web for research.

*Curriculum Resource: Lesson Plan—Using the Web for Research in the Elementary Classroom*

## ELEMENTARY SCHOOL EXAMPLE OF AN ONLINE RESEARCH PROJECT

### Getting Started

**Scenario:** You are a reporter who has just arrived in Seattle in 1898. You and your partner have decided to start a local newspaper. Your task is to create a newspaper page that includes articles, advertisements, pictures, and other elements that are reflective of the time period.

**Guiding Question:** What was life like in Seattle during the Gold Rush of 1898?

### Steps in the Research Cycle

**Questioning:** Reintroduce the guiding question: What was life like in Seattle during the Gold Rush of 1898?

Assist students in generating subsidiary questions, such as: What was the housing situation? Why did people leave for the Klondike from Seattle? What was the economic base? What were the roles of women? What was the impact of the Gold Rush on the Native Americans?

**Planning:** Have teams develop a plan for tackling questions. This includes a plan for note taking and identifying potential types of resources. You may provide students with a "research record" or graphic organizer that will help organize information.

**Gathering:** Have students use books, maps, and other library resources, as well as Web sites, to gather information.

**Sorting/Sifting:** Once a variety of information has been gathered, have students organize information into potential categories for use in the newspaper.

**Synthesizing:** Create a storyboard of the newspaper layout. Plan for the newspaper articles and write drafts. Have students ask themselves if they have enough information.

**Evaluation:** Have students ask themselves if their newspaper has enough information and if it matches with the time period.

**Reporting:** Have students share their newspapers with each other. This may include posting them within your classroom Web site.

## Assessment

**Evaluation:** Develop a rubric that assesses the content of the articles within the newspaper, the product (such as the visual design of the newspaper), and the process—group collaboration and steps within the research cycle.

**Learnings:** The ISTE NETS Technology Foundation Standards include:

### Standard 3. Research and Information Fluency

- Students apply digital tools to gather, evaluate, and use information.

### Standard 5. Digital Citizenship

- Students understand human, cultural, and societal issues related to technology and practice legal and ethical behavior.

(International Society for Technology in Education, 2007).

*Curriculum Resource: Lesson Plan—Using the Web for Research in the Secondary Classroom*

## HIGH SCHOOL EXAMPLE OF AN ONLINE RESEARCH PROJECT

### Getting Started

**Scenario:** You have been appointed to one of several special federal government committees that have been asked to review our current presidential election process and make recommendations to members of a House and Senate subcommittee regarding potential election reform. You and your team will utilize the research cycle to develop a recommendation, based on historical research and current events, as to whether election reform is in order.

**Guiding Question:** What factors influenced the configuration of our current election system?

## Steps in the Research Cycle

**Questioning:** Reintroduce the guiding question: What factors influenced the configuration of our current election system?

Assist students in generating subsidiary questions, such as: What is the electoral college? Why was the electoral college developed? What are problems and positives associated with the electoral college? What are the problems with our current voting system? Are any populations marginalized within our current system?

**Planning:** Have teams decide roles and responsibilities, and a plan for gathering the initial information. This should include a process for sharing information with each other. Students should also be encouraged to develop an information organizer before starting the process.

**Gathering:** Have students use online resources, including online newspapers, in addition to library and classroom resources.

**Sorting/Sifting:** Students should continually meet and organize information.

**Synthesizing:** As a group, students should process initial answers to their questions and lay out potential recommendations. Determine if more information is needed.

**Evaluation:** When enough information is collected, students should organize their presentations.

**Reporting:** Each group of students will present its case to another group of students (such as a different class), who will then decide which recommendations they would accept. They should create visuals utilizing available technology and resources.

## Assessment

**Evaluation:** Rubrics should be created that evaluate the process (including following the research process and participation), the content of the presentation (are the recommendations based on a logic that follows from their questioning and information gathered), and finally for the presentation materials and delivery (the product).

**Learnings:** The ISTE NETS Technology Foundation Standards include:

### Standard 1. Creativity and Innovation

- Students demonstrate creative thinking, construct knowledge, and develop innovative products and processes using technology.

### Standard 2. Communication and Collaboration

- Students use digital media and environments to communicate and work collaboratively, including at a distance, to support individual learning and contribute to the learning of others.

### Standards 4. Critical Thinking, Problem Solving, and Decision Making

- Students use critical-thinking skills to plan and conduct research, manage projects, solve problems, and make informed decisions using appropriate digital tools and resources

(International Society for Technology in Education, 2007).

*Curriculum Resource: Web Sites*

The Bellingham School District, located in Bellingham, Washington, has created online investigations based on the research cycle and requires one to be completed every year starting at Grade 3. Their online investigations with full lesson plans and guidelines for the development of each stage are available at: http://www.bham.wednet.edu/studentgal/onlineresearch/newonline/online.htm. In addition to this site, we suggest that you visit http://questioning.org/module/module.html, which provides a step-by-step process for how you can create your own online research modules that help your students develop their research and critical-thinking skills.

## INTEGRATING THE WEB INTO THE CURRICULUM: SPINNING THE WEB (PRODUCTION)

The Web can be a powerful tool for presenting and distributing classroom projects. Students can use the Web to demonstrate their understanding of content and standards. The multimedia nature of the Web allows students to demonstrate their creativity and understanding by providing the option to go beyond text to include images, sounds, and video. Projects created by students can be distributed to the teacher, other students, parents, or the general public. Teachers can also use the Web to create projects and resources that can be shared with their students, parents, other teachers, or the general public. The Web sites created by students and teachers can be posted to a public server for everyone to see or kept more private by keeping the projects on a disk or computer hard drive at school in order to control access.

The process for creating an actual Web site is described in detail in Chapter 3. What follows is a look at how to successfully managing your students through the process of creating a Web project. The following two examples demonstrate the use of this Web project creation process.

## The Web as a Multimedia Project: Managing Multimedia Projects in the Classroom

Spinning the Web in the classroom is a multimedia production project similar to many others. It can be a long-term activity like the school newspaper, the school play, and the school yearbook, or a short-term one like a book report or classroom presentation. Successfully managing student multimedia projects in the classroom takes a great deal of planning and organization. By following proven guidelines, teachers can incorporate student-generated Web projects into the curriculum to help students learn content and meet content standards.

Guidelines for managing classroom multimedia projects[1]:

- *Set clear expectations for the Web-based project.* What do you want your students to accomplish? What are the objectives of the project? Be realistic with the available time, classroom resources, and the skill of your students. Also, be clear with how they will be evaluated. What exactly are you looking for in the project? We discuss this in detail in the "Evaluating Student-Generated Web Projects" section of this chapter.
- *Develop a production calendar/schedule.* Work with students to develop a schedule for when different elements of the project are due. This will help to keep them on task and help ensure the project will be completed on time.
- *Have students start the project on paper.* Have students brainstorm and sketch out what they will be accomplishing before they start developing their project on the computer (this process is often called

---

1. The Clearing House, *Teaching Students to Critically Evaluate Web Pages, 75*(1), September and October, 2001. Reprinted with permission of the Helen Dwight Reid Educational Foundation. Published by Heldref Publications, 1319 18th Street, NW, Washington, DC 20036-1802. www.heldref.org. Copyright © 2001.

storyboarding). It's easier to make changes to paper sketches than it is to change a completed Web page. Sharing paper-and-pencil sketches gives young producers an opportunity to receive constructive criticism and to make design changes before they invest time in spinning their Web pages.

- *Provide instruction in using the tools.* Provide instruction on how to use the production tools (e.g., word-processing software, HTML editors, scanners, digital cameras), as needed. In any classroom, a few students usually have some experience using one or more of the tools available. Build in opportunities for students to work with each other, along with providing teacher-led training and support. Ideally, you will build a community of support for your students where they do not have to rely solely on you for help.

- *Manage the classroom resources.* Resources, especially technology resources such as computers, digital cameras, and so forth, can be scarce. Develop a schedule that allows students or student groups to have access to different resources at different times.

- *Monitor student progress.* Meet with students frequently to monitor their progress and provide feedback. Have students peer-review their work. Student feedback can be beneficial, especially if students have had this feedback appropriately modeled for them by their teacher.

- *Provide time to share completed projects.* Web projects can be shared with a larger audience by placing the projects on a server where others can access the project, if they are provided the Web address (URL). Students tend to work very hard on computer-based multimedia projects and are often excited to show what they have accomplished. This is a great way for them to also share what they have learned.

---

*Curriculum Resource: Guidelines for Managing Classroom Multimedia Projects*

- Set clear expectations for the Web-based project.
- Develop a production calendar/schedule.
- Have students start the project on paper.
- Provide instruction in using the tools.
- Manage the classroom resources.
- Monitor student progress.
- Provide time to share completed projects.

## Student-Generated Project Example Ideas

The following two lesson plan examples show how students can create Web projects that demonstrate their understanding of content and standards. Each lesson is meant to be carried out over multiple days. The exact number of days would vary, based on the available resources you have and the technology skill of your students. Keep in mind that your students would be creating actual Web sites—by either hand coding or using an HTML editor (see Chapter 3). You could have your students use a blog or wiki (these tools are discussed in Chapter 1) to share their understanding of content and standards. It is important to note, however, that when students use these tools they are not "spinning the Web" (that is, creating their own Web site); students are simply using Web tools that allow them to manipulate content that can be viewed on the Web.

---

*Curriculum Resource: Lesson Plan—Student-Generated Web Project—Elementary School*

**Lesson Plan: Fourth Grade Social Studies**

**Background:** Fourth grade students in California study the geography of the state. They learn to use maps, charts, and pictures to describe the similarities and differences among communities within the state.

The state's History–Social Science standards that address this are[2]:

4.1   Students demonstrate an understanding of the physical and human geographic features that define places and regions in California.

4.1.3. Identify the state capital and describe the various regions of California, including how their characteristics and physical environments (e.g., water, landforms, vegetation, climate) affect human activity.

4.1.4. Identify the locations of the Pacific Ocean, rivers, valleys, and mountain passes and explain their effects on the growth of towns.

---

2. Adapted from *History-Social Science Content Standards for California Public Schools (Kindergarten Through Grade 12)*. © 2000, California Department of Education.

4.1.5. Use maps, charts, and pictures to describe how communities in California vary in land use, vegetation, wildlife, climate, population density, architecture, services, and transportation.

The ISTE National Educational Technology Standards and Performance Indicators for Students (revised June 2007) include:

### Standard 1. Creativity and Innovation

- Students demonstrate creative thinking, construct knowledge, and develop innovative products and processes using technology.

(International Society for Technology in Education, 2007).

A well-planned Web production lesson would meet both of these standards.

**Goal:** To have students increase their understanding of the similarities and differences among regions and communities within the state of California through the organization and articulation of their existing knowledge, as well as new information gained through research. The students will accomplish this organization and articulation by planning and producing a Web site on the subject.

**Objectives:** Students will decide how best to present the information by designing a Web site. Students will produce a simple Web site that uses text and images to describe at least four different California communities.

**Activities:** Working individually or in teams students:

- Gather and organize information about the different communities.
- Design the necessary Web pages. If the design includes more than one page, students will also design a navigation scheme for the pages.
- Write appropriate text for the Web site.
- Gather graphic images (maps, charts, and pictures) and format them for the Web. This may require locating, creating, or modifying images, as well as formatting images into Web-readable .jpg or .gif files.
- Produce the pages based on the designs created. They will incorporate the text and media elements (images) into HTML files using either a Web editor or word-processing software producing HTML code.

**Evaluation:** Students will be evaluated on their participation in the design and production process (this includes evaluating their gathering and organizing information for the site). The site contents will be evaluated for accuracy of information and clarity of communication. The final product (the Web site) will be evaluated.

### Lesson References

California State Board of Education. (2005). *Content standards.* Sacramento, CA: Author. Retrieved June 30, 2007, from http://www .cde.ca.gov/be/st/ss/

International Society for Technology in Education. (2007). *Educational Technology Standards for Students*, Second Edition.

---

*Curriculum Resource: Lesson Plan—Student-Generated Web Project—High School*

### Lesson Plan: Eleventh Grade English

**Background:** High school students in New Jersey are expected to develop skills in both the writing process and basic applications of technology. New Jersey's Core Curriculum Content Standards state that by twelfth grade, students should engage in the following[3]:

#### Language Arts Literacy

1. Writing as a Process (prewriting, drafting, revising, editing, postwriting)
   a. Engage in the full writing process by writing daily and for sustained amounts of time.
   b. Analyze and revise writing to improve style, focus and organization, coherence, clarity of thought, sophisticated word choice and sentence variety, and subtlety of meaning.
   c. Review and edit work for spelling, usage, clarity, and fluency.
   d. Use the computer and word-processing software to compose, revise, edit, and publish a piece.

---

3. Adapted from *New Jersey Curriculum Content Standards for Language Arts Literacy and Technology Literacy,* © 2000, New Jersey Department of Education.

   e. Use a scoring rubric to evaluate and improve own writing and the writing of others.
   f. Reflect on own writing and establish goals for growth and improvement.

### Technological Literacy

1. Basic Computer Skills and Tools
   a. Produce and edit page layouts in different formats using desktop publishing and graphics software.
   b. Develop a document or file for inclusion into a Web site or Web page.
   c. Discuss and/or demonstrate the capability of emerging technologies and software in the creation of documents or files.
   d. Merge information from one document to another.

**Goals:** To design and develop a Web site that allows students to share their writing with a "real" audience of peers in a public forum. Students will increase their understanding of the draft and revision processes by receiving feedback from the teacher and from their peers. Students will develop a better understanding of how the Web works by posting their work to a Web space and responding to works posted via e-mail or Web-based forms. Students will develop a better understanding of the importance of designing a site that is well organized, operates reliably, and is easy to understand.

**Objectives:**

- Students will design and develop a Web-based literary magazine that showcases their class's writing.
- Students will "publish" student-written essays, poetry, or short fiction on this class Web site.
- Students will design a method for providing feedback to other students' writing via e-mail or Web-based forms. (Students will use this feedback to revise their work.)

**Activities:** The teacher will present the project to the entire class, explaining the goal of the site (to publish student work). The teacher holds a discussion, gathering input from students on how the site should be organized and what it should generally look like. Students are then assigned specific tasks, working alone or in small groups, including design, organization, editing, and production.

Once tasks are assigned, students work independently or within their groups to complete their tasks (students who are not directly involved in design and production at various times may work on their own writing pieces). The teacher should encourage students to keep the site design simple, reminding them that they have a limited amount of time in which to produce the site and that its primary goal is to showcase student writing.

After the site is up and running, members of the class will post their work for peer review and feedback (the site might be divided into two sections: one for works-in-progress and one for final drafts). Students may be assigned the role of "site editor," responsible for maintaining the site, uploading new writing pieces, and removing older drafts (this might be a role assigned to a number of students on a rotating basis).

**Evaluation:** The process of site design and development can be evaluated. The final product (the site itself) can be evaluated. The content of the site (students' individual writing pieces) can be evaluated.

**Lesson Reference:**

New Jersey State Department of Education. (2004). *New Jersey core curriculum content standards*. Trenton, NJ: Author. Retrieved June 30, 2007, from http://www.state.nj.us/njded/cccs/

*Curriculum Integration Idea: Another Example of Student-Generated Web Projects*

The ThinkQuest Competition (http://www.thinkquest.org/) is a long-term, extracurricular Web production project that is popular in schools around the world. Sponsored by the Oracle Education Foundation, ThinkQuest is a project-based activity in which students work in teams to build creative and educational Web sites that explore globally relevant subjects. The competitions are open to students and teachers from anywhere in the world. Each team must have three to six students who are between the ages of 9 and 19, and one adult coach who is a school employee. There are three age divisions: 12 and under, 15 and under, or 19 and under. Teams have to build a Web site on any topic within one of a range of official competition categories. ThinkQuest encourages people to form diverse teams made up of members from more than one school, community, or country. Competition entries are evaluated in a two-step process that includes peer review and judging by an international panel of professional educators.

Completed Web sites are published in the ThinkQuest Library for the world to see. Winning teams travel to ThinkQuest Live, a prestigious awards event in San Francisco, California, to celebrate their achievements.

## INTEGRATING THE WEB INTO THE CLASSROOM CURRICULUM: COOPERATIVE LEARNING ACTIVITIES

Cooperative learning is an instructional strategy in which students work together in small groups of three to five students to achieve a common goal. As students work together, they are not only responsible for their own learning, they are also responsible for the learning of those in their group. Cooperative learning has proven to be an enormously effective instructional method (Johnson & Johnson, 1999; Sharan, 1999; Slavin, 1994). The integrating of the Web with cooperative learning can provide effective learning activities that can assist students in learning content and in meeting content standards.

Following are two examples of lessons that combine the use of the Web with cooperative learning. Students are in groups of four, and each student has a unique role that must be carried out if the group is to be successful. The first lesson is for a high school U.S. history course and could be completed in one 55-minute class session. However, it also could be spread over additional days, depending on your students' skills. In this lesson, the Web is used to provide students with access to primary source photographs that most likely are unavailable in the classroom. The major objective of the lesson is to teach students how to analyze photos.

The second example lesson is designed for upper elementary students. As with the previous lesson, the Web is used to provide access to information that is not available in the classroom. The goal for students is to create a travel brochure for a particular city within the United States.

*Curriculum Resource: Lesson Plan—High School Lesson Using Cooperative Learning and the Web*

### PRIMARY SOURCES: ANALYZING ARTIFACTS

High School—History 55-minute class session—could be expanded to multiple class sessions

**Materials Needed:** Primary source images—can be of any historic event. Two great sites to find images are:

1. Library of Congress (http://memory.loc.gov/ammem/index.html). This site provides links to various primary source images and documents dealing with United States history.

2. Smithsonian Institution (http://www.smithsonianeducation.org/ educators/index.html). You will need to search the site for various images that fit your needs.

**Alignment With Standards:** Florida Social Studies Standards (Grades 9–12): Note—this lesson could fit with various social studies content standards, based on what is being taught. We have included a more generic social studies standard. Standard 1 (SS.A.1.4): The student understands historical chronology and historical perspective: (4) Uses chronology, sequencing, patterns, and periodization to examine interpretations of an event.

Florida Language Arts Standards (Grades 9–12):

Standard 2 (LA.B.2.4): The student writes to communicate ideas and information effectively: (4) Writes text, notes, outlines, comments, and observations that demonstrate comprehension and synthesis of content, processes, and experiences from a variety of media.

ISTE National Educational Technology Standards for Students:

**Standard 3. Research and Information Fluency**

- Students apply digital tools to gather, evaluate, and use information.

**Objectives:**

- Students will be able to critically analyze a primary source photo by describing different elements of what they believe is taking place.
- Students will be able to make predictions of the historical period of an artifact.

**Lesson Process:** Primary Instructional Method Used: Cooperative Learning

### A. Focus/Motivation

Begin by showing a picture (or another artifact) to your students. Have them first look at the picture before answering the following question: "What do you think is taking place in this picture?" After allowing them to think about it for about 30 seconds, have them turn to a neighboring student and share their responses. Let about a minute pass before allowing different pairs to share with the entire group—take volunteers.

Once this has taken place, describe to your students that you can find out about certain time periods in history by analyzing artifacts and making conclusions based on the artifacts.

### B. Lesson Process

Divide students into groups of three. Give each student a specific role: (1) scribe, (2) presenter, and (3) Web researcher. Provide each group with a photo; we suggest giving out several different photos. The task for each group is to analyze the artifact (photo) to determine what was going on during the time period the photo was taken. Have students answer who, what, when, where, and why. Have each group make a prediction about their photo before they gather support that either supports or refutes their predictions. Allow time in class for groups to use what resources they have to complete this part of the assignment. Have students search the Web for evidence.

The scribe will write down the predictions and the data evidence that the group discovers. The Web researcher will help lead the group through searching the Web for evidence to support or refute their predictions. The presenter, as the name implies, will share with the class what the group found out. Give each group about two minutes to share.

### C. Closure

Summarize what took place. Remind students of the purpose of analyzing artifacts. Historians use analysis and prediction to learn about historical periods.

**Evaluation:** You should evaluate the content, product, and process of this assignment. This lesson could be evaluated by observing how your students interact and what they report in their presentations. You could make it more formal by creating a rubric and having the group turn in the work that they created.

**Variations to the Lesson:**

1. Use a historic photo of a scene such as a city street. Have students provide an oral description of the sights, sounds, and

smells that make up the scene in the photo. Students should provide evidence from the photo and other sources about the time period the photo was taken. Students should examine the photo to locate clues about the economics of the time.

2. Select a historical photograph. Have students predict what they believed happened one minute and one hour after the photo was taken. Have your students explain the reasoning behind the predictions they made.

*Curriculum Resource: Lesson Plan—Elementary School Lesson Using Cooperative Learning and the Web*

## STATE POSTERS: EXPLORING THE UNITED STATES

Social Studies—Fourth Grade Multiple Class Sessions

**Materials Needed:** Construction paper, computer printer, glue, tape, scissors

**Alignment With Standards:**

Michigan Language Arts Standards (Later Elementary):

Content Standard 2: All students will demonstrate the ability to write clear and grammatically correct sentences, paragraphs, and compositions.

Michigan Social Studies Standards (Later Elementary):

II—Geographic Perspectives: (2) Locate and describe diverse kinds of communities and explain the reasons for their characteristics and locations; (3) Locate and describe the major places, cultures, and communities of the nation and compare their characteristics.

ISTE National Educational Technology Standards for Students

**Standard 3. Research and Information Fluency**

- Students apply digital tools to gather, evaluate, and use information.

**Objectives:** Students will be able to analyze and synthesize information found on the Web to create a travel poster about a U.S. city.

**Lesson Process:** Primary Instructional Method Used: Cooperative Learning

### A. Focus/Motivation

Show your students various travel brochures and posters (note: you can often get these from a travel agent). Ask them to look the materials to see what is in common. Have them share with a neighboring student what they think the posters have in common. After about a minute, have them share their answers with the entire class. Share with them that travel posters and brochures attempt to generate excitement that leads to individuals taking a trip to that location.

### B. Development

Put your students into groups of four. Give them the roles of: (1) illustrator, (2) writer, (3) editor, and (4) presenter. The illustrator will be responsible for creating the illustrations or locating the pictures for the poster. The writer will be responsible for the text that goes on the poster. The editor is responsible for editing the text. The presenter will present the poster to the entire class. All of the students will be researchers for this project. Each will also be responsible for physically putting the poster together.

Tell your students that they will be creating their own travel posters of a city in the United States. The posters need to include illustrations and text that talks about the attractions of the city. The poster will take several class sessions to complete. (An alternative to the poster is a PowerPoint presentation.)

1. Allow students time to search on the Web. 50states.com (http://www.50states.com/) is a great site to have them start their research. They must first select a city (a capital city is a great choice). They will need to decide what is interesting about their city that will attract people to come visit it.

2. The group will need to write text for the poster.

3. The group will need to either create their own images or find them on the Web (if you have a printer they can print them).

4. They will need to put the poster together. They should create a layout for the poster before tapping or gluing the text and images on the construction paper or poster board.

### C. Closure

Have students share their travel posters with the group.

**Evaluation:** We believe it's important to evaluate the content, product, and process of this assignment. A rubric can be created that deals with specific elements of the project, such as the content presented, the poster quality, and the quality of the presentation. You should also evaluate how well the group worked together. The exact elements you feel are important about this project should be included in the rubric.

## INTEGRATING THE WEB INTO THE CURRICULUM: PROBLEM-BASED LEARNING ACTIVITIES

Problem-based learning is an instructional strategy that promotes active learning through the development of solutions to real-world problems. It's characterized by the following elements (Barrows, 1996; Stepien & Gallagher, 1993).

- *Reliance on problems to drive the curriculum.* Problems do not test skills and knowledge; rather, they assist in the development and refinement of skills and knowledge.
- *Ill-structured problems.* Problems presented to students are not intended to have one solution. As new information is gathered by students, perception of the problem, and thus the solution, will most likely change.
- *Students solve the problems.* The role of a teacher is as a coach and facilitator.
- *Students are provided guidelines only for how to approach problems.* There is no one method for how students should approach a given problem.
- *Authentic, performance-based assessment.* Assessment is a consistent and transparent part of the learning process.

---

*Curriculum Integration Idea: WebQuest*

The Web is a great resource that can be integrated into a problem-based learning (PBL) environment. A frequently used and well-researched approach to using the Web in a K–12 PBL environment is a WebQuest. A WebQuest is completely Web based—the instruction/activities are presented on a Web site that has been created in advance, and students typically only use the Web as they engage in the WebQuest. It's important to note that not all WebQuests can be considered PBL activities; many of them are, however. We suggest that you visit the WebQuest site to view various WebQuests that teachers have created for different content areas and grade levels. Visit http://www.webquest.org/ and select *Find WebQuests,* which is a link on the left of the site. You will be taken to a WebQuest search page.

---

*Curriculum Integration Idea: Monarch Butterfly Project*

There are many other examples of how the Web has been used in a PBL approach. One that we like is the Monarch Butterfly Project. The major goal of this project has been to monitor the migration of monarch butterflies, something that requires the cooperation of classrooms around the country. There have been different approaches to how best to accomplish this goal. You can visit various sites that show how this has been accomplished. We recommend the following ones:

- http://www.learner.org/jnorth/
- http://www.monarchwatch.org/
- http://www.education-world.com/a_curr/curr023.shtml#tracking

ThinkQuests, Webquests, and tracking butterfly migration are only a few of many Web-based learning activities. As we have pointed out, these activities can range in purpose from research to media production and can be applied to individual students working on extracurricular projects to entire classes working cooperatively. The Web is a truly powerful teaching resource.

## EVALUATING STUDENT-GENERATED WEB PROJECTS

Although Web projects can take on various forms, the primary goal for using the Web in the classroom remains the same—to help students learn content and meet content standards. It's important to keep this in mind as you develop your evaluation protocols, because the use of technology can often overshadow the content, leading to more emphasis being placed on the product students create than on the content. Even though content should be the most important element, the product students create and the process they go through in creating the product are important as well. A well-designed evaluation protocol, therefore, will take into consideration all three areas: content, product, and process.

## Our Approach: Content, Product, Process

Incorporating all three areas of a Web project into an evaluation protocol can be tricky at first. However, it is not impossible, and it becomes quite natural the more you integrate student Web projects into your curriculum.

---

### Curriculum Resource: Rubric—Evaluation Protocols

Let's take a closer look at content, product, and process, and then examine two evaluation protocols that include all three.

- *Content.* We do not profess to be content experts in all the subject areas that are taught in K–12. Therefore, we will leave you with the task of determining what elements you feel are most important in helping establish whether your students understand the content. One idea we will pass along, however, is that in our current educational climate where standards are a major focus, it's important to make sure that you have adequately addressed content standards. You must be able to demonstrate how Web projects are tied to helping your students meet content standards. Without this connection, it will be difficult to support spending the time it can require to have students engage in Web projects.
- *Product.* Earlier in this chapter we focused on using the Web for research and production projects. Your evaluation protocol will differ slightly depending on which of these two types of projects you have your students complete. For example, the resulting product of a production project will be a Web page. Your evaluation protocol would need to address issues of functionality and design of the Web page that students create. If you had your students use the Web for a research project, this would not be the same. The product, most likely, would be a paper or presentation that detailed the ideas they discovered. The evaluation protocol for this project would focus on the elements of a well-written research paper or clearly delivered speech. You could, of course, have them share their results of the research as a Web page. In this case, you would also want to include issues of functionality and design as part of the evaluation protocol.
- *Process.* In most classroom environments, resources are limited, which necessitates having students share scarce resources. One method for having students share resources as they participate in a Web project was discussed earlier in this chapter; this

method is cooperative grouping. Placing students in cooperative groups requires that students not only share resources, they also share responsibilities for helping create the final product. Each student takes on a specific role and function that must be carried out if the final product is to be successfully completed. As you develop your evaluation protocol, we suggest including elements that allow you to determine how well your students worked together. Two ways of evaluating process that we use are observation and student reflection. Observation allows us to view our students as they work through the production process— on an individual level and as a part of a group. Student reflection provides the opportunity for each student to evaluate how well he or she worked as part of the group, and how well their group members functioned (from the student's perspective). Unless you practice self-reflection with your students and model appropriate behavior, you may not get the results you desire. We believe it is extremely important to clearly indicate your expectations of their behavior. Students will participate in meaningful self-reflection and evaluation of peers, if it's done in a safe and caring environment.

## Web Project Evaluation Rubric Examples

The following three examples of evaluation rubrics can be used with your students. We hope these examples help you generate ideas on how you can develop your own rubrics that evaluate the learning that takes place with your students.

The first rubric example is what we call a *plus/minus* rubric that allows you to evaluate the product, process, and content of a Web project your students create. We use a 100-point scale. The first category determines whether students have met the minimum requirements for the project by completing all of the necessary elements. Students would receive a score of 70 for this. If students have not met the 70-point requirement, we typically give them the opportunity to do so (however, this would be your decision). The remaining categories should receive either plus or minus points. For example, if all aspects of their Web projects worked without errors they would receive 5 points. If one of their hyperlinks (Web links) didn't work, they could only receive 4 points. Students with multiple errors in this category could actually lose points. The points gained in each category in the rubric would be added to or subtracted from the 70 points to arrive at the overall grade for the Web project. We provide this rubric to our students at the beginning of each project so they understand exactly how they are being evaluated. You could change the categories to include other items or to be more detailed. The focus, however, should remain on the three categories: product, process, and content.

Student: _____

| Product Project (+/–) Grading Based on 100-Point Scale | |
|---|---|
| Completion of all assigned tasks | 70 points |
| All aspects of project work correctly | 5 points +/– |
| Project tested by others | 5 points +/– |
| Thoroughness of preproduction activities (script, storyboards, etc.) | 5 points +/– |
| Content is accurate and complete | 5 points +/– |
| Neatness, spelling, grammar, and organization | 5 points +/– |
| Group worked together effectively | 5 points +/– |
| Comments: | |
| Total Points | |

*Rubric*: Web Project Evaluation Protocol

## Curriculum Resource: Rubric—Web Research Project: Traditional Rubric Example

The second example is a more traditional rubric. The rubric is used to evaluate Web research projects conducted by fifth grade students. Five different categories are being evaluated, and each category is graded on a 1-through-4 scale—with 4 being the highest. The total points possible for the project would be 20.

Student: _____

| | 1 | 2 | 3 | 4 |
|---|---|---|---|---|
| **Information** | Information presented is inaccurate and/or incomplete. | Information presented is accurate but not complete. | Information presented is accurate and complete. | Information presented is accurate, complete, and presented in a unique way. |
| **Organization** | There is no logical organization for the paragraphs. | Some paragraphs are logically organized. | Most paragraphs fit together in a logical manner. | All paragraphs fit together in a logical manner. |
| **Grammar and Spelling** | More than five grammar and/or spelling errors. | Three to five grammar and/or spelling errors. | One or two grammar and/or spelling errors. | No grammar or spelling errors. |
| **References** | Citations are not provided. | Citations are provided for a few references. | Citations are provided for most references. | Citations provided for all references. |
| **Presentation Quality** | The product has multiple errors. | The product has several errors. | The product has few to no errors. | The product is error free and is presented in a creative manner. |

Total Points: _____

Web Research Project: Traditional Rubric

*Curriculum Resource: Rubric—Web Project*
*Evaluation Protocol: Student Checklist*

The third rubric example is designed to help guide students as they create their own Web projects. We would not necessarily use this rubric to directly evaluate our students. Students would use it to make certain they have included all of the required elements of a particular project. The rubric is a checklist that guides them through the development process.

---

☐ All necessary elements included in the project?

☐ Grammar and spelling checked?

☐ Is the content you included accurate?

☐ Have you included references for work you have cited?

☐ Do the links work?

☐ Is the navigation easy to use?

☐ Does the media work—images, audio, video?

☐ Have you made sure that the media file sizes are not too big?

☐ Does each page have a title?

☐ Have you been consistent in the layout and design of our project?

☐ Have you tested your project on more than one computer?

☐ Have you had someone else use the project to test it?

---

Web Project Evaluation Protocol: Student Checklist

## ADDITIONAL WEB RESOURCES: TAKING SMALL STEPS

Now that you have read through these project and lesson activity examples, you still might not feel like you are ready to implement a full-blown lesson or project that integrates the Web into the curriculum. This is not a problem. With practice and experimentation, you will get to the point where integrating the Web into your curriculum will be something you do with no worries.

As we mentioned early in the book, you should start out integrating the Web in small steps. The Web is full of sites that can provide resources that you can immediately use in your classroom. These resources can be starting-off points for you to begin integrating the Web in your curriculum. As you gain more confidence, you can move on to more complex projects and activities like those described in this chapter.

The following is a brief list of some of our favorite sites you can use to take small steps to using the Web in your teaching. Keep in mind that the

Web is a dynamic environment—sites can change and often do. Some of these sites may no longer exist or may have changed locations. Putting the key terms in a search engine or index (such as Google) can provide you with other helpful sites. We suggest you conduct a search of your own to find your own hidden gems!

- *Creating Graphs and Charts* (http://nces.ed.gov/nceskids/). This site allows you to create various charts and graphs by inputting data. This is a great tool to use to show students various ways to graphically organize numerical data—like results from an experiment or class survey. If you have a projector attached to your computer, you can display the graph or chart to your entire class.
- *Maps of the World* (http://www.lib.utexas.edu/maps/). Various sites provide great images of maps. One of our favorites is from the library of the University of Texas at Austin. They have an online collection of various maps organized in numerous ways. One method for organization is by current interests. You could have your students visit this site to view different maps as part of a social studies lesson or to explore a geographic area they have read about in language arts or a literature class.
- *The World Factbook* (https://www.cia.gov/cia/publications/factbook/index.html). This site links to the CIA World Factbook, which provides a wealth of information about every country in the world. It's a great source of data for you and your students to learn more about issues such as the official language of a country or even the number of Internet users in a country.
- *Digital History* (http://www.digitalhistory.uh.edu/). Many excellent sites provide access to digital copies of primary sources in history. One of our favorites is Digital History. Not only does it provide access to primary sources, it provides links to other Web sites on history. Digital History primarily focuses on United States history.
- *Virtual Museums and Libraries* (http://www.sil.si.edu/). The Web provides access to the collection and resources of many of the world's most well-known and important museums and libraries. One of our favorite sites is offered by the Smithsonian Institution Libraries. You can access a variety of media—mostly images and audio—that can enhance your curriculum. The site provides resources that can be used in science, social studies, the humanities, and the arts.

- *The National Library of Virtual Manipulatives* (http://nlvm.usu.edu/en/nav/topic_t_2.html). This site is maintained by the University of Utah. The purpose of the site is to provide students with the opportunity to explore math concepts using "virtual manipulatives." The site provides math activities that explore concepts from basic math, data analysis, to geometry for students in grades kindergarten through the twelfth grade.

## SUMMARY

The goal of this chapter is to demonstrate how the Web can be integrated into the curriculum. It included several examples that we hope provide you with guidance as you develop lessons that utilize the Web in the classroom. We emphasized two types of Web-based projects—research and production—and provided an effective process for teachers to guide students as they develop Web-based projects in the classroom. In addition, the chapter described how the Web can be integrated with cooperative learning and PBL activities to help students learn content and meet content standards.

This chapter included a discussion on evaluating the Web sites and student projects. Evaluation is a key element to consider as you integrate the Web into your classroom as a teaching and learning tool. We approached evaluation in two different ways. The first is teaching your students the skills to critically evaluate the Web sites they visit to determine if the information presented is valid and reliable. The goal is to help students become discriminating consumers of Web site content. Our approach to accomplishing this is based on a series of questions we like to teach our students to answer about a Web site. As you become more comfortable with using the Web in your classroom, we suggest that you develop your own unique approach that meets the specific needs of your students.

The second approach we focused on is evaluating student-generated Web projects. Often when students use technology in the classroom, the product they create overshadows the content. As you develop your evaluation protocols, be aware of the emphasis you place on various elements of these projects. Learning content and meeting standards should be the focus for your students. Although this should be the major focus, the product students create and the process they go about in creating the product are also important. Our approach in evaluating student-generated Web projects, therefore, includes evaluating all three areas: content, product, and process.

## GOING BEYOND THE CHAPTER

### 1. Develop Lesson Plans That Integrate the Web.

The purpose of this chapter was to provide you with practical ways in which you can integrate the Web into the curriculum to help your students to learn content and meet standards. Identify at least one area of your curriculum where you can develop two lessons that use the Web. As you develop your lessons, keep in mind the different concepts and ideas that have been presented in this chapter. Make sure that you have included strategies for how you will evaluate your students' learning.

### 2. Visit the Telementoring Web Site.

To learn more about telementoring, we suggest the article at the following link about the effectiveness of using telementoring in the K–12 classroom. A PDF version of the article can be found at http://www.ncolr.org/jiol/issues/PDF/1.1.6.pdf.

### 3. Visit the NoodleTools Web Site.

An excellent Web site that can help your students narrow down where to start their search for research on the Web is NoodleTools, which can be found at http://www.noodletools.com/debbie/literacies/information/5locate/adviceengine.html. We suggest visiting this site to see the various Web sites that your students can use to conduct research.

### 4. Develop Your Own Web Site Evaluation Form.

Your task is to develop your own Web site evaluation form. After reading through this chapter and its examples, conduct a Web search to find sites that have different kinds of evaluation forms. The purpose is to read enough samples to generate ideas that will help you create a form that meets the unique needs of your students. We suggest you start with Google (http://www.google.com/) and use various terms in your search such as *Web evaluation form* and *evaluating Web sites.* Keep in mind that you will need to be critical about the Web sites you visit because, as you have found out in this chapter, not all Web sites are created equal. You will need to employ the skills you will teach to your students to discriminate among the sites!

**5. Develop a Rubric.**

Your task is to develop a rubric for a Web project you will integrate into your curriculum. Use one of the examples discussed in this chapter as a guide. Remember to keep in mind that you should include content, product, and process as categories you will use to evaluate your students.

# Solving the Mystery of Designing and Creating Web Sites

## GUIDING QUESTIONS

This chapter will help you answer the following questions:

- What is HTML?
- What are the essential elements of every Web page?
- How does a browser "read" a Web page?
- How does a browser find Web pages on the Internet?
- What is a Web server?
- What is Web editing software?
- How is a Web site made available for the world to see?
- What are the steps involved in designing and producing a Web site?
- What is the difference between a Web page's function and its form?
- What are the unique characteristics of the Web as a medium?
- How much control does a designer have over the way an end-user will see a Web page?

## KEY TERMS

| | |
|---|---|
| Browser | Function |
| FTP | HTML |
| Form | Layout |

| | |
|---|---|
| Markup Language | Tag |
| Mock-ups | Web Editing |
| Navigation | Software |
| Scrolling | Web Server |
| Source Code | WYSIWYG |

## OVERVIEW

Now that you have an understanding of what the Web is and how it works, and you have seen how it can be integrated into the curriculum, we want to help you venture out into creating your own Web sites. This chapter explains how to make Web pages and how to make those pages viewable worldwide. It explores the essential elements of a Web page and the basics of putting those pages someplace that allows for people all over the world to access them. We begin by examining the coding language (HTML), the building blocks of a Web page, then look at the ways browser software interprets that coding and how browsers find pages. This chapter finishes with an introduction to Web servers and the fundamental processes involved in making your own Web pages available for public view.

You will see how to go about designing and developing a Web site, from first idea to finished product, and how to make pages that are easy to read and have visual appeal. We begin by describing a simple, three-step process for Web design and development, then describe what makes the Web different from other media.

After reading this chapter you will be able to make a Web page from scratch, using a simple word processor, without having to rely on complicated and sometimes expensive Web editing software. We show you how to incorporate graphics into a Web page and how to link your page to other Web pages, as well as what's involved in making that page a part of the Web.

This chapter outlines the production processes involved in creating Web pages and sites. You will understand the unique characteristics of the Web as a medium of communication, and will be able to apply the principles of linking, navigation, and layout to your own Web pages.

---

### Why You Need to Learn HTML

Imagine how you might feel if you were a talented storyteller who wanted to put the stories down on paper, but you could not write. Others might write your stories for you, but you could not edit them or make changes without the writer's help. Trying to make a Web page without understanding HTML is like that—if you don't understand the principles of HTML you will never have real control over your Web pages.

As professors of educational technology, we have taught dozens of courses that involve Web page creation, and for a number of years we have studied how teachers approach making Web pages. Almost every teacher participating in the technology education classes that we examined started out by attempting to design overly complicated Web sites (they wanted to design sites that included opportunities for online chat and test feedback). The vast majority of these teachers also stated that they would use Web editing software (usually FrontPage and Dreamweaver) to complete these tasks, without realizing the cost of the software, the time necessary to learn to use the software, or the fact that no Web editing software works perfectly (one almost always has to adjust what the software creates by manually changing some HTML). Few of the teachers we studied could describe HTML or the basic workings of the Web. These teachers did not understand the basics of Web page construction, and few of the teachers could find school support for Frontpage or Dreamweaver. When teachers relied on templates ("ready made" Web page designs that allow one to insert personal information in a few areas), the resulting projects looked impressive, but the teachers could not make any changes to the page to suit their specific needs. Teachers who use Web editing software or Web templates without understanding HTML are at the mercy of the people who created the software and the templates.

## Professional Responsibility

According to the International Society for Technology in Education's (ISTE's) *National Educational Technology Standards for Teachers* (NETS-T), all teachers need to "demonstrate a sound understanding of technology operations and concepts" (NETS-T 1). Furthermore, all teachers need to "demonstrate continual growth in technology knowledge and skills to stay abreast of current and emerging technologies" (NETS-T 1B). To understand the operations and concepts of Web page creation, you must understand what HTML is and how it works.

Teachers who understand HTML have far more control over the Web pages they create. If Web editing software does something "funny" to a Web page, the teacher who knows HTML can fix the problem. A teacher who knows HTML does not have to rely on templates created by others. A teacher who knows HTML is fulfilling a professional obligation to keep abreast of current technologies and has tremendous power over the Web environment.

## Knowledge Is Power

A problem teachers face when they express interest in making Web pages is that many things conspire to suggest that Web pages are easier to make if one uses software and supports created by others instead of learning HTML, the basic principle of Web page creation. Schools have become more adept at incorporating sophisticated Web technology into their programs, using learning management systems such as Blackboard, or using templates that allow teachers to fill in a form and perhaps upload a picture to create a personal space on the school Web site. These are all wonderful supports for making the Web a useful means of communication among teachers, parents, and students, but they do very little to help one gain true control over making Web pages.

If you understand the basics of HTML, you will gain true mastery of the Web; if you don't understand HTML basics, you will be continually in need of help from people who do. Furthermore, learning HTML helps you in your "continual growth in technology knowledge and skills." The best news of all, though, is that HTML is not difficult to learn.

## HTML: THE LANGUAGE OF THE WEB

Hypertext Markup Language, or HTML, is actually quite easy to learn. It's not a programming language like JAVA or C+ (which take a great deal of time to master), and most people learn HTML very quickly. HTML is a *markup language*, which means that it isn't programming per se; it's more like making format notes that indicate how you want the words to look when a person views them using a browser (e.g., Internet Explorer or Netscape). HTML is the oldest method of making Web pages (as opposed to newer markup languages like XML). HTML is a little limited, which is why other methods of making Web pages were created, but it has the advantage of being easy to learn and easy for just about any computer with browser software to interpret correctly. To make Web pages that contain words, pictures, and perhaps a little video or sound, a command of basic HTML is all you need.

HTML is a collection of *tags* that help you format your work. A tag looks like this: <font size="16">. It's called a tag because the less-than and greater-than signs at the beginning and end make it look like the kind of tag you might see attached to items in a store. In a way, HTML tags work the same way as store tags do because they give specific information about the item they are attached to. Here are some common HTML tags:

```
<i>              "italicize the text"

<b>              "make the text bold"

<font size="16">  "set the font size to 16"
```

HTML is easy to type using word-processing software. Any word processor will do, but we find the simplest ones are the best because they do not try to reformat your work (for example, Microsoft Word does not make it easy to create a simple HTML file; you often see quite a few extra letters and symbols thrown in when trying to view the file on a browser). When we teach HTML in a classroom, we use the simplest word-processing software on the computer: on a PC, Notepad or Wordpad; on a Macintosh, Simpletext or TextEdit. Using the simplest possible word-processing software will ultimately make things much, much easier as you learn to "spin" Web pages.

---

### They Call It *Spinning*

People who work with Web pages regularly refer to creating them as *spinning* pages. For obvious reasons, arachnid jokes abound in the world of the Web.

---

For now we will work under the assumption that you are *not* using any Web editing software (such as Macromedia Dreamweaver or Microsoft FrontPage). You really don't need these to make Web pages and, although you may find them helpful later on as you get more involved in making larger and more sophisticated Web sites, it's actually better to start by making Web pages without the aid of these software packages. You will be amazed at how much you and your students can create using simple word-processing software. Even more important, you will be able to fix the small problems that invariably arise when using Web editing software because you will understand the basics of HTML at the "source code" level. After you become familiar with HTML, using Web editing software will be particularly helpful, and we introduce the more popular editing programs toward the end of this chapter.

## Source Code

The collection of tags and words that comprise a Web page is called its *source code*. This is a very techno-sophisticated sounding term, but all it really means is "here is how the page looks before a browser makes use of the tags." For example, here is a little bit of source code:

```
<b>This is bold text!</b>

<P>

<i>And this is italic text!</i>
```

The <P> is a *paragraph* tag; it means, "start a new paragraph." Most tags require an end tag (for example, </i>) to indicate when that particular formatting should stop. The slash (/) character inside a tag indicates an end. When the browser interprets this source code it looks like this:

**This is bold text!**

*And this is italic text!*

The source code is everything that has been typed by the person creating it to get the Web page to look a specific way for the person viewing it.

---

### Peeking at Other Web Pages' Source Code

You can view the source code of any Web page. Browser software like Netscape and Internet Explorer invariably provides an easy way to see the HTML tags used to create the page that is displayed on the screen. In Internet Explorer, select the pull-down menu "View," then select "Source." In Netscape, select "View," then select "Page Source."

---

### What Exactly Is a Browser?

We have mentioned *browser* software a number of times. We have even used the specific examples, Internet Explorer and Netscape. Let's review the term *browser*—one more time. If you have ever looked at, well . . . *anything* on the World Wide Web, you have used browser software. A browser is any software that translates source code into formatted text. A browser interprets HTML tags, using them to arrange text and organize images in the browser window in a very specific manner. Browsers do not *create* Web pages; they allow one to *view* Web pages.

There are a number of popular Web browsers and each has slightly different capabilities and strengths; all of them, however, can interpret basic HTML. The most popular browsers are currently Internet Explorer and Netscape. Others that have gained popularity include Firefox (http://www .firefox.com), Opera (http://www.opera.com), and Safari (http://www .apple.com/safari/download/—Safari is specifically for Macintosh computers); these are free to download from their respective Web sites. If you are going to create Web pages, it is a good idea to keep a few different browsers on your computer so that you can check to be sure that your Web pages look appropriate no matter which browser is being used to view them.

Figure 3.1 shows what the browser displays and the HTML source code used to create that display.

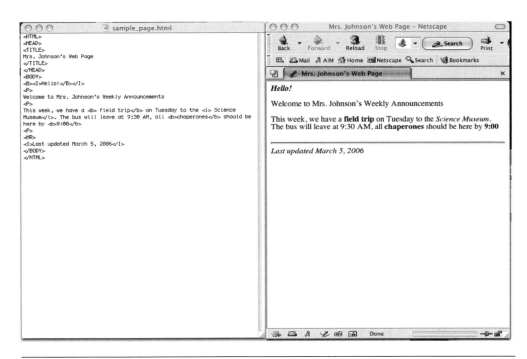

**Figure 3.1**    A Side-by-Side View of a Web Page and Its Source Code

The left side of Figure 3.1 is what was created in TextEdit software (basic word-processing software on a Macintosh). The right side of Figure 3.1 is that source code interpreted by the Netscape browser.

To summarize everything so far, HTML is used to make Web pages. HTML is a set of tags that indicate format and arrangement. The HTML tags and text used to make a Web page is called its source code. Browser software interprets the source code to display a Web page the way its author intended, with none of the tags showing.

## MAKING A WEB PAGE

Making a Web page is quite easy once you know the procedure. Let's start with a quick explanation of the terms *HTML file* and *Web page.* For our purposes these two terms are synonymous. A Web page *is* an HTML file and vice versa. HTML files always end in either *.html* or *.htm*. The only way a browser can read an HTML file is if the file names ends with *.htm* or *.html*. We cannot stress this enough: as soon as you create the file, name it something that ends in *.htm* or *.html*. For example *starthere.html* and *page_two.htm* are valid file names that a browser will interpret as a Web page. Files without an *.htm* or *.html*, such as files named *mygreatWebpage* or *mypage.doc* will *not* be recognized by a browser.

---

### .html or .htm: Is There a Difference?

Back in the early days of computing, PC operating systems could only accommodate what was known as a "dot-three extension." File types (the letters after the dot) had to be three characters. HTML files were therefore labeled *.htm*. Later, when file extensions could be longer, people switched over to *.html*. Today both *.htm* and *.html* are considered valid extensions. Neither one is considered better to use than the other.

---

## Naming Files

Naming HTML files that will be interpreted by multiple computers and browsers is a little trickier than naming files that will only be read on your computer. Remember that your HTML files have to be read and interpreted by any computer connected to the Internet. There are some conventions to follow that will ensure that your files are readable by everyone. Of course the file name must end in either *.htm* or *.html*, but following a few other rules will help your files get read properly no matter what computer views them. The first rule is *no blank spaces*. Do not put a blank space anywhere in the file name (for example *my page.html* is a must-to-avoid). If you are using multiple words, use an underscore character to link them together (e.g., *my_page.html* will work). Some characters should be avoided when naming files, including *?*, */*, and *$*—these characters are used in programming to denote very specific situations and can cause problems if they are used in a file name. Also, avoid using the period character (.—everyone calls this a *dot*) anywhere but just before the file extension. A less critical concern but worth mentioning all the same is to avoid using numbers to start a file name or as a complete file name (for example, *1page.html* and *1123.html*). Finally, avoid using capital letters; stick with lowercase letters and numbers for file names.

| Good | Bad |
|------|-----|
| my_file.html | my file.html |
| file1.htm | file.1.htm |
| myfile.html | myfile.txt |
| file_1.htm | File_1.html |
| file_1.html | 1_file.html |

**Figure 3.2**     Examples of Good and Bad File Names

## The Essential Formatting of a Web Page

All HTML files begin and end with the tags <HTML> and </HTML>. All HTML files have a *head* and a *body*, which are marked by the <HEAD></HEAD> and <BODY></BODY> tags. For example, let's look at the source code from Figure 3.1:

```
<HTML>

<HEAD>

<TITLE>

Mrs. Johnson's Web Page

</TITLE>

</HEAD>

<BODY>

<B><I>Hello!</B></I>

<P>

Welcome to Mrs. Johnson's Weekly Announcements

<P>

This week, we have a <b> field trip</b> on
Tuesday to the <i> Science Museum</i>. The bus
will leave at 9:30 AM, all <b>chaperones</b>
should be here by <b>9:00</b>

<P>

<HR>
```

```
<I>Last updated March 5, 2006</I>

</BODY>

</HTML>
```

Notice where the <HTML> and </HTML> tags are placed (at the beginning and end of the code sequence). Notice how the <HEAD></HEAD> and <BODY></BODY> tags are placed (they mark the beginning and ending of the head and body sequences). The head sequence is where information is placed that will not be seen in the browser window (in our example, the only information in the head sequence is the *title*, which appears as a label above on the outer edge of the browser window). The body sequence is where information is placed that will be seen within the browser window (in our case, the word *Hello!* and the information about this week's field trip).

---

**Tag Format**

HTML tags are not case sensitive. You can use either uppercase letters or lowercase letters when creating tags. You can place tags on their own lines or type one long continuous, left-to-right line; the browser will simply read each tag as it comes to it, it doesn't matter whether they are each on their own line, in one continuous line, or some combination of the two. We recommend giving each tag its own line (similar to the example in Figure 3.1), especially when learning to write HTML. This will make it easier to see what you are doing and easier to proofread and troubleshoot your work later on.

---

### Try Spinning a Web Page!

After reading this far in the chapter, you should be able to create your own Web page. So, try it out! Set the book up next to your computer and complete the following tasks:

1.  Open Notepad, Wordpad, Simpletext, or TextEdit (virtually every Windows-based or Macintosh computer has one of these on it).

2.  Type the following:

    ```
    <HTML>

    <HEAD>
    ```

```
<TITLE> My Page </TITLE>

</HEAD>

<BODY>

<P> This is my Web page! It is the
beginning of many wonderful pages
to come. </P>

</BODY>

</HTML>
```

> In this area, you can type anything you want. Remember to use <P> tags when you want to start new paragraphs.

3. Save the file as *my_page.html* (keep in mind the italics are *not* necessary, they are just for emphasis in this book). If you save it to the desktop it will be particularly easy to locate in Step 4.

4. Open any browser on your computer (e.g., Internet Explorer, Netscape, or Safari). From your browser, select "Open File" (usually found in the "File" pull-down menu) and choose the file you have just created (you will probably select "browse" to find the file on your computer).

5. You should now see your Web page displayed in your browser!

You see, we told you creating a Web page was easy! The basic components to every Web page are the <HTML>, <HEAD>, and <BODY> tags. With these in the correct place and a proper file name (one that ends in *.htm* or *.html*) you can create simple Web pages very quickly. Creating more elaborate pages is just a matter of knowing which of the many HTML tags to use to get the format you want.

## More Tags

We recommend a number of resources that cover HTML tags extensively at the end of this chapter. In this section we list and describe the tags we find teachers use most often. This is a brief and selective list of the multitude of valid tags, but we think you will find these to be the tags that are critically important to a basic Web page.

### Aligning the Elements of a Page

You can use tags to control the alignment of the items on a Web page. Items can be either be centered, left justified, or right justified. The tags that make this happen are pretty easy to remember:

```
<CENTER>  </CENTER>
```

Everything after the <CENTER> tag and before the </CENTER> tag will be centered horizontally within the browser window.

```
<LEFT>  </LEFT>
```

Everything after the <LEFT> tag and before the </LEFT> tag will be aligned to the left within the browser window.

```
<RIGHT>  </RIGHT>
```

Everything after the <RIGHT> tag and before the </RIGHT> tag will be aligned to the right within the browser window.

### Formatting Text

As we have seen, text can be formatted using tags.

```
<B>  </B>
```

Everything after the <B> tag and before the </B> tag will be displayed as bold.

```
<I>  </I>
```

Everything after the <I> tag and before the </I> tag will be italicized.

```
<P>
```

Anything after the <P> is a new paragraph (some people add the </P> at the end of each paragraph, but this isn't necessary).

```
<FONT SIZE=" "> </FONT>
```

This will change the type size to whatever is specified within the quotation marks. For example to make the type size 18 point, the tag would be <FONT SIZE="18"> (if you do not add the </FONT> tag, all the text for the rest of the Web page will be 18 point).

```
<FONT COLOR=" "> </FONT>
```

This will change the color of the font to whatever is specified within the quotation marks. See the box titled "Specifying Color in HTML" to learn more about what to put within the quotation marks.

To change the font color and size, put everything together in one FONT tag. For example, to make text that is 20 point and green, use the tag <FONT SIZE="20" COLOR="GREEN">. Use the </FONT> tag to return the font to its default size and color.

```
<BLOCKQUOTE> </BLOCKQUOTE>
```

This will indent the text on both sides in a way that is typically used for quotations. It is very effective for making a paragraph or passage stand out from the rest of the text.

### Making Links to Other Web Pages

One of the great strengths of the Web is the ability to link pages to pages in other places. All you need to know is the *URL* (universal resource locater) or the *address* of the page you wish to link to. For example, the URL or address of the Google search engine home page is http://www.google.com/.

```
<A HREF=" "> </A>
```

Use these tags to create a link from your page to another Web page. For example the source code <A HREF="http://www.louvre.org/"> The Louvre Museum</A> will create a link that looks like this, <u>The Louvre Museum</u>, and when clicked will take the user to the Louvre Museum's Web site.

```
<A HREF=" " TARGET="BLANK"> </A>
```

Add TARGET="BLANK" to your link tag to have the link open in a new window. Having a link open in a new window keeps the original Web page open (for example, if students "wander off" to the Louvre, then to the Prado and then to the Metropolitan Museum of Art, they can still see your Web page in a separate window the entire time they are wandering).

> ### The Fine Art of Linking Web Pages:
> ### Absolute and Relative Paths
>
> All Web pages have a unique URL, also called a Web address. For example, the URL or address for *The New York Times* on the Web is http://www.nytimes.com/. This is known as an *absolute path* name because there is only one HTML file with this address on the entire Web, and the address is a complete one (that is to say it begins with *http://*).
>
> When you are making Web pages that will link to each other, and you don't know yet what each page's absolute path name will be, you can use a *relative path* name; that is, the name of the file itself. For example, you can link my_page_1.html to my_page_2.html by using the file name itself. You can only use relative path names when all the files reside in one directory (or are nested in directories within one main directory, but this takes some practice with slash dot syntax , using the / and . characters to navigate within the directories—we recommend avoiding slash dot syntax until you have more practice spinning Web pages).
>
> Use absolute path names for pages on other Web sites that you wish to link to. Use relative path names when linking the pages of your own Web site.

### Adding Graphics to Web Pages

As you have seen from your own Web surfing, many pages have pictures on them. Graphics cannot be directly inserted into an HTML file, but the HTML file can make space for a graphic file that the browser will display within the same window as the HTML file. Browsers can display three types of graphic files: .jpg (or .jpeg), .gif, and .png (this means the image file has to be formatted as one of these file types and that the file name has to end in *.jpg, .jpeg, .gif*, or *.png*). For the image to show correctly, the graphic file has to reside somewhere the browser can find it. It's a good idea to place the graphic file in the same directory as the HTML file that uses it and to use a relative path name to call that file.

```
<IMG SRC=" ">
```

IMG SRC is short for *image source.* Place the name of the graphic file you would like to display within the quotation marks. For example, the tag that allows the display of a picture of a rubber duck (a file named *duck.jpg*) is <IMG SRC="duck.jpg">.

```
<IMG SRC=" " HEIGHT=" " WIDTH=" ">
```

To control the size of the image you can add HEIGHT and WIDTH to the tag. Place the number of pixels you want the image to be within the quotation marks that follow HEIGHT and WIDTH.

### Changing the Color of the Background

The background color of an HTML page is gray by default. Some browsers automatically change the default color to white, *but some browsers do not.* To control the background color of your Web page, you make an adjustment to the <BODY> tag.

```
<BODY BGCOLOR=" ">
```

Instead of a <BODY> tag, use the <BODY BGCOLOR=" "> tag. Place the name or the hexadecimal notation of the color you would like to use within the quotation marks. See the box titled "Specifying Color in HTML" to learn more about how to name colors. For example, to make a page that has a white background, use the tag <BODY BGCOLOR="white"> or <BODY BGCOLOR= "# FFFFFF">.

---

**Specifying Colors in HTML**

There are two methods of specifying colors in HTML. The simplest way is to use the name of the color. However, only sixteen colors can be called by name: aqua, black, blue, fuchsia, gray, green, lime, maroon, navy, olive, purple, red, silver, teal, white, and yellow. A much wider array of colors are available by using hexadecimal notation. Hexadecimal names of colors look like this: #000000 (this is black) or #FFFFFF (this is white). Hexadecimal color names are the # sign plus six characters between 0 and F (0, 1, 2, 3, 4, 5, 6, 7, 8, 9, A, B, C, D, E, F: sixteen possible characters, hence the name hexadecimal). The first two characters are the value for red, the next two are the value for green, and the last two are the value for blue (red, green, and blue are the primary colors of light). 0 is the lowest value for that color and F is the highest. For example, #FF0000 is bright red while #660000 is a pale red or pink. Hexadecimal color code charts are very easy to find on the Web (try using the phrase *HTML color* in any search engine).

### The <HR> Tag

A nice little visual component of a Web page is the *hard rule*—a horizontal line that looks as if it is etched into the background. This is an easy and elegant-looking way to separate information on a Web page. All you need to do is place the tag <HR> wherever you want a horizontal line.

### Putting It All Together

With a little practice using these tags, you and your students can create some pretty nifty Web pages using nothing more than a simple word processor. As with anything, the more you practice the better you will get with HTML. Best of all, when you are ready to begin using Web editing software like Macromedia Dreamweaver or Microsoft FrontPage, you will be able to troubleshoot formatting problems because you can understand and edit the source code.

## WEB EDITING SOFTWARE

Now that you know how to work in HTML, it's time to consider Web editing software. Web editing software makes Web page creation easier by adding all the tags "behind the scenes"—in other words, with Web editing software you get a *WYSIWYG* experience. WYSIWYG (pronounced *whiz-ee-wig*) is the acronym for "What You See Is What You Get." Web editing software is a WYSIWYG experience because you can work on creating a Web page without having to see or type the tags; the software puts all the tags in place while you work on a page that looks like the finished product.

Web editing programs are similar to word-processing programs. Using a Web editor feels very much like using a word processor, but its main function is to place HTML tags in the correct place. The industry standard is currently Macromedia's Dreamweaver. A thirty-day free trial version of Dreamweaver is available at http://dreamweaver.adobe.com/. A Web editor that is pretty good and completely free, Nvu, is available at http://www.nvu.com and is very similar to Dreamweaver for purposes of making Web pages. A variety of other Web editing programs are available; you will need to experiment with a few to decide for yourself which one is right for you.

What we particularly like about Dreamweaver and Nvu is that they both allow you to switch between a view of the page as it will look through a browser and a view of the source code that you can edit. Most Web editing software makes Web page creation easier, but no Web editor is perfect. There will be times when you have to edit the source code itself to get exactly what you want, and that's why we provided an introduction to source code and tags before discussing Web editing software. With a little knowledge of how tags work and the basic structure of HTML, you can make great use of Web editing software to create Web sites.

## VIEWING WEB PAGES: HTTP

While HTML is the markup language that allows us to make Web sites, HTTP (Hypertext Transfer Protocol) is what allows us to *see* Web sites. Browser software uses HTTP to display Web pages that are stored on remote computers. A complete Web address usually begins with *http://*. The *://* is the techno-symbol for "invoke" (as in "start using"). So the address, http://www.washingtonmiddle.edu/jonesclass.html is telling the computer to "invoke HTTP to display the Web page located on the Washington Middle School Web server; specifically the Web page named *jonesclass.html.*" When we say *Web server* we are referring to a computer that's connected to the Internet for the purpose of making things like HTML files available to the general public. A Web server generally runs all the time so that people can access the files on it whenever they want. People access Web files on a server using browser software. For example, typing *http://www.google.com/* into the address line of any browser running on a computer connected to the Internet will cause the browser to display the *default page* of the Google Web site.

### Default Pages

Of course the question anyone would ask after reading the previous paragraph is: "What the heck is a default page?" You will notice that a Web address such as http://www.google.com/ does not end in *.htm* or *.html*—it looks as if it's not specifying a Web page to view. Default pages are those HTML files that automatically display from a Web server directory if no specific HTML file is designated. There are specific ways you have to name the default page, depending on how the Web server is configured. The most common default page names are *default.html, home.html,* and *index.html,* but you would have to ask the person in charge of a specific Web server which one to use for that server. In other words, when you type *http://www.google.com/* into the address line of a browser, it will display the *index.html* file located on the Google Web server. If a Web server has a default page set up and running, then every directory (a directory is like a folder where a bunch of files are kept together) can have a default page. This is why it's often possible to surf the Web for quite a while before seeing a Web address that actually ends in a file name.

### Viewing Web Pages Locally
### (Viewing Files That Are on Your Computer)

If you tried the *spin your own Web page* activity earlier in this chapter, you already know that HTML files that reside on your computer can be viewed through browser software running on that computer. Because these files are not available through a Web server, the browser simply "invokes the file." When you select a file that resides on the same computer as the browser, instead of *http://* you will see *file://* in the address bar of the browser. For teachers, there are two things that are important about this bit of information:

1. You can view your HTML files in a browser before making them public. In this way you can make sure everything looks the way you want it to before putting the work on worldwide, public display.

2. You and your students can make Web pages that can be viewed only in the classroom. This is a good thing to keep in mind if you wish to make use of copyright-protected materials (which teachers may use following the guidelines of *fair use* only in a classroom, not on the World Wide Web). This is also a good thing to keep in mind if safety is a concern, as in the case of creating Web pages with students' photographs and names—this is not something you would want to make publicly available.

Keep in mind that other, remote computers cannot access HTML files residing only on your computer. To give the world access to your files, you must put them on a Web server.

## SHARING YOUR WEB SITE WITH THE WORLD

Creating a Web site that can be viewed by the entire world requires that you put all the files used for the site (all the HTML and graphics files) on a Web server. As you no doubt recall, a Web server is a computer that's dedicated to the task of making the files it holds available to anyone connected to the Internet.

You will most likely create your Web pages on your own computer, which is not a Web server (it's possible to make your own computer act as a server if you leave it on and connected to the Internet all the time, but we do not recommend it). You will then need to transfer all the HTML and graphics files that make up your site to a Web server. The trick is finding an easy way to make the transfer.

## Sending Files to a Web Server: FTP

The most common method of transferring files from your computer to a remote one is via *FTP*. FTP stands for *File Transfer Protocol*. As discussed in Chapter 1 (and in the Resources), all protocols are standardized forms of communication among computers. This standardization means that *all* computers can understand each other at this level. The FTP allows users to send and receive files via the Internet. To send your files to a remote server, all you need is to have the computer you are working on connected to the Internet. FTP can be invoked a number of ways, depending on your computer's operating system or software you have available. The easiest way we know of is to use a software program dedicated specifically to FTP. Because we cannot know what kind of computer you are using, we will make a few very sweeping, generic recommendations about FTP software. Your best bet, however, is to consult with your school or district's technology specialist to find out if the district can recommend and support a particular method of FTP.

If you are completely on your own with no technology support, we advocate using FTP software that's simple and cheap. The best way to find this is to use a reputable online, downloadable software database. Our favorite one of these databases is *Tucows* (http://www.tucows.com/); we like the fact that all the software available is rated on a five-cow scale. More important, we like that the site is well kept and easy to navigate, and all software is checked for viruses before it's made available. We also like *Download.com* (http://www.download.com/), another respectable and safe place to obtain software. A large number of good FTP software titles can be downloaded for free from these sites. We recommend typing *FTP* into the search line for these sites and selecting the FTP software that is both the highest rated for your computer's operating system and available free of charge.

All FTP software works in the same manner. The software usually offers you two windows: one is the list of files on your own computer; the other is the list of file directories (folders) available to you on the Web server. You select the files you want to *upload* from your computer and the place you want to put them on the Web server. Most often it's just a matter of clicking a button marked "upload" once you select the files and their destination.

To send files from your computer to a Web server, FTP software will ask you to establish a connection between your computer and the remote server. Often there is a command labeled *connect* or *connect to* that you activate to start this process. To connect you will need some information about the Web server: you will need to know things such as the server's address (something like *http://www.schoolserver.edu*), as well as your account name and password. These are all things that the people who run the Web server you use will have to provide for you.

### Finding Server Space

Some schools or districts provide Web server space for their teachers. Some do not. It's up to you to locate the server spaces you have at your disposal.

If your school or district provides server space for teachers, it's just a matter of finding out how to access that space. You will need to find who the *Webmaster* is; that's the person who controls and maintains the server. We recommend you become friendly with the Webmaster, as she or he can be a great source of information and support.

If your school or district doesn't provide server space for teachers, you will need to find space on a commercial server. This isn't as daunting as it might sound; a number of reasonable options are available to someone who is willing to do a little detective work.

#### Commercial Server Spaces

In the quest for server space to call your own, the first thing to consider is which groups you may belong to that provide its members with space as a courtesy. If you subscribe to an *Internet service provider* (ISP), such as America Online or EarthLink, you have server space as part of your membership. If you use a cable modem at home, the cable company may also provide you with server space as part of its service.

If you do not have access to server space through any subscriptions or groups you belong to, it is possible to find free space on the Web. Web *hosts* allow you to post your files on their Web server, but they usually incorporate advertising into your site (either with pop-up Web pages or a banner inserted into the top or bottom of your Web pages). Free hosting services can be useful if you have no other options, but you must be careful to find out in advance what type of advertising your site will be displaying. Using the phrase "free Web host" in any search engine will give you a huge number of hosting options to choose from.

One of the benefits of using a commercial server space is that it's often maintained by sophisticated, professional Webmasters. These sites often have FTP functions built into them that allow you to transfer your files without having to use separate FTP software.

## DESIGNING AND DEVELOPING A WEB SITE

Making a great-looking Web site may seem like a daunting task, but it's actually a very manageable and rewarding process if you take it one step at a time. Web site development is essentially a three-step process:

1. Decide what the Web site will do.

2. Decide what the Web site will look like.

3. Produce the Web site.

You may find it surprising, but the first two of the three steps are accomplished largely without the use of a computer! Like most design projects, the biggest challenges are met using paper and pencil, a bit of creativity, and the application of problem-solving strategies.

## Step 1: Decide What the Web Site Will Do

The very first thing you need to do is decide what purpose your Web site will serve. Designers refer to this as the site's *function*. You probably already have a number of ideas about the kind of site you want to make; now you need to think specifically about who will be looking at your site and exactly what its content will be. Although it's human nature to think in broad terms at the beginning of any design activity, the best designers refine their thinking extensively before anything gets produced. The purpose of this first step is to clarify your thinking about your site in order to make it suit your needs and the needs of those using it.

---

### Sites and Pages: What's the Difference?

People often use the terms *Web site* and *Web page* synonymously. True Web aficionados know the difference. A Web page is a single HTML file; a Web site is the collection of all the HTML files (pages) that make up a single, cohesive grouping of information. For example the San Diego Zoo Web site (http://www.sandiegozoo.org/) is a large collection of Web pages, all of which are created and maintained by one organization. A Web site may, however be comprised of a single HTML file, in which case it would be correctly referred to as either a site or a page.

---

As you develop your idea of a Web site, see how many of these questions you can answer:

- Who do you hope will look at your site? What kinds of people do you want to attract? How old are they? What is their level of education? What is their experience with using the Web?

- What information does your site provide? Is your site meant to be informational or is it meant to be entertaining? Is the information provided vitally important to your audience or is it more for their personal enjoyment? How many topics and subtopics will you divide the information into?
- Will the information on the site change frequently? How often will the information need to be changed? If the information needs to be updated regularly, where will the update information come from and who will keep the site up to date?

Creating detailed answers to these questions should help you refine your thinking about the purpose of your site. These questions may also serve to help you change your thinking about your site. For example, it may sound wonderful to have a site that will have new information posted every day, but answering the question "Who will keep the site up to date?" may cause you to reconsider your original idea. At this point in the design process, you should be thinking solely about the site's function. Think about who will use the site and what they will use it for; also consider the resources available to support and maintain the site. In the second step, you will use this information to decide what each page of the site will actually look like.

## Step 2: Decide What the Web Site Will Look Like

Once you have decided the site's function, you can begin to sketch out what each page of the site will look like. Designers call this determining the site's *form*. At this point, it is very tempting to begin making actual Web pages—resist this temptation! The problem with making Web pages at this point is that once you have created a page, it's very difficult to think of making significant changes—and if you start making links to other pages, it becomes an especially daunting task to make changes to all the pages that are linked to each other. During this step in the process, it's far better to make paper-and-pencil sketches in order to decide how the finished pages will look.

Paper-and-pencil sketches, known more commonly as *mock-ups*, give you an opportunity to "mess around" with different ideas in a way that isn't too time consuming. It is much easier to make a sketch of a Web page than it is to generate the source code for one. Best of all, you can mark up the sketch with notes and changes in seconds, or even throw away the sketch entirely without feeling that you have invested a lot of time creating an HTML file. We recommend making a sketch for each page of the

Web site showing where the graphics and text will be placed and how they will be grouped together on each page. Remember, these sketches are working drafts; not many people will see them so they do not have to be well-crafted or pretty, but they should be detailed enough to serve as a blueprint for the actual Web pages.

**Figure 3.3**     An Example of a Mock-Up Sketch

In most cases a Web site is comprised of multiple Web pages. If this is true for your site, you will want to decide in advance how these pages are linked together. Along with your page sketches, you may want to make a *navigation chart*. A navigation chart is a graphic display of how the Web pages in a site are linked to each other. One of the easiest and most efficient ways to make a navigation chart is to use Post-it Notes and paper. Have each Post-it stand for a specific Web page, then place them on a large sheet of paper and draw lines that indicate the options a person has for going from one page to another. A completed navigation chart will show you exactly what links have to be on each page. We describe navigation and navigation strategies later in this chapter.

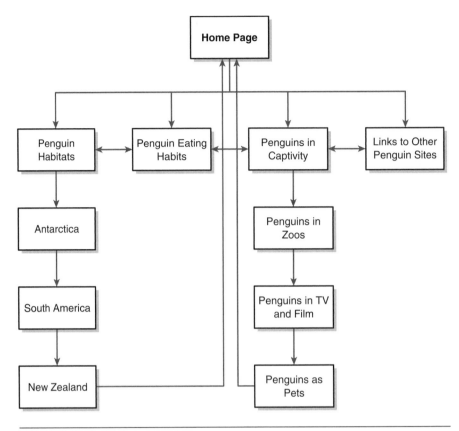

**Figure 3.4**    An Example of a Navigation Scheme (created with Inspiration software)

### Step 3: Produce the Web Site

If you approach Steps 1 and 2 thoughtfully and thoroughly, the third and final step is relatively simple. At this point, all you have to do is make the pages themselves, using the blueprints you have provided for yourself in the first two steps.

Start by gathering together all the media elements you plan to incorporate into the site. This is a matter of collecting, creating, or modifying any graphics files you plan to use (you may be using sound or video as well; this is a bit more advanced, but you still have to gather all the files you are going to use). Put together all the content information you will be using as well. If you are using a lot of text, it's probably easier to work with it using your favorite word-processing software. You can then cut-and-paste the text from the word-processor file into the HTML file.

**Web Design and Cooperative Learning**

The processes involved in developing Web pages make wonderful classroom cooperative learning activities (see Chapter 2 for examples of cooperative learning and the Web). Students can work on the design and development of Web pages in teams, and each team member can assume a specific role (for example, project manager, writer, artist, or fact checker). Because most of the design and development is accomplished with paper and pencil, cooperative teams can work quite well even if computers are only available to them for a limited amount of time. Groups following this three-step process should be able to make best use of computer time, because they have accomplished most of the design and development through the creation of paper mock-ups.

## DESIGNING WITH THE WEB'S UNIQUE CHARACTERISTICS IN MIND

Deciding first what a product will do, then deciding what it will look like, and finally making that product is a common approach to the design of just about anything. The Web, though, has some unique properties that you will need to keep in mind as you decide what your site will look like. Think of the Web as a medium. We are using the term *medium* to mean a type of mass communication. For example, radio, television, and newspapers are each a communication medium, each with its own distinct characteristics. Each medium has its own strengths and weaknesses. In planning your Web site, the trick is to design your pages with the strengths of the medium in mind.

The Web is a medium that is unlike traditional print and different from other broadcast media such as television or radio. It's even fundamentally different from most other types of computer software. It's a unique environment, and there are some special considerations that you should keep in mind when you design and produce Web pages.

### Everybody Sees the Web a Little Differently

People access the Web on a variety of different computers. These computers have different-sized monitors that may be set to different resolutions. A number of different browsers are used to view the Web as well, and individuals have idiosyncratic preferences when it comes to the size of the window they use for the browser display. When designing for the Web, keep in mind that your pages will be seen in a lot of different ways, depending on the viewer's computer, monitor, software, and personal preferences.

*Tech Talk: Screen Resolution*

Computer screens display information as a series of little rectangles called *pixels* (a truncation of the term *picture element*). These pixels are very small, individual blocks of color. The number of pixels per square inch of a screen display is called the *resolution*. Different screens have the ability to show more or fewer pixels. Older screens typically can show a total of 307,200 pixels (640 pixels wide by 480 pixels high). Newer screens can show many more pixels, and resolutions of 1,024 wide by 768 high (786,432 pixels) are quite common.

Here is the strange part: the larger the number of pixels, the smaller the image! This is because the more pixels there are, the smaller each pixel is, making an image look like it's smaller and in sharper focus on a screen with a high resolution.

The fact that everybody views Web pages using different hardware and software means that you have to keep your page designs simple if you want them to be viewed correctly as often as possible.

## Choosing the Right Font

For a beginning Web designer, the right font is the *default* font. On the Web, the default font is *Times*, 12 point (if you don't specify a font or a font size, you will automatically get 12 point *Times*). You can specify other fonts when you generate the source code for your HTML files, *but you cannot know if that font is available on another person's computer.* The fonts available on a computer depend on what has been loaded into that computer's operating system. If one uses a font called Gothic Rock 'n Roll Engraved when making a Web page, the only people who will see that text correctly are others who have the Gothic Rock 'n Roll Engraved font loaded into their operating system (and we can tell you right now the number of people who have this font is very small!). When a font is not available to a computer, that computer usually makes use of another font that it has in its operating system as a replacement. The result can be at best mildly confusing or ugly, and at worst completely incomprehensible.

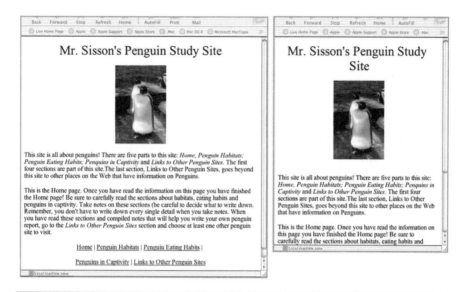

**Figure 3.5**    The Same Web Page Viewed in Two Different-Sized Browser Windows

There are ways of specifying a font and supplying that font via the Web, but accomplishing that is very advanced Web work and not something we recommend at this time. It is far easier and more reliable to simply stick with the default font.

Limiting yourself to the default font does not have to mean limiting your creativity. You can specify the font size and color, and whether it is bold or italicized. Use a larger size, a different color, and perhaps bold or italic options to make headlines that stand out from the rest of the text.

## Scrolling

If your Web page has a great deal of content to it, the chances are very good that not all of it will be visible to the viewer all at once. It's quite common to have to *scroll* down a page, and Web surfers usually don't find this problematic. While most people consider scrolling up and down to be quite reasonable, scrolling from left to right (or right to left) is another matter entirely. Most people find left/right scrolling on a Web page to be inappropriate and unattractive.

Regular text is not a problem here. Unless it's specially formatted, text will automatically *wrap* itself to fit the left/right dimensions of a browser window. The thing to watch out for is graphic images. Be sure to use images that are small enough to fit into a typical-sized browser window's left/right dimensions (if you keep your images under 600 pixels wide you should have very few problems).

## Links

Links are one of the Web's unique features, and one of its most powerful assets. As you have learned in this chapter (and no doubt know from your own Web surfing experiences), you can use HTML to create links from one Web page to any other Web page. This allows the user to create a very personal experience as he or she surfs the Web.

The problem with links is that they can lead off in almost any direction, taking the user away from your site and off to any of a thousand other possibilities. For example, your site on oceanography might have a link to the Discovery Channel's Web site, which might have a link to CNN's site, which might have a link to the Cartoon Network's site . . . before you know it, your students have stopped looking at oceanography and focused their attention on the *Powerpuff Girls!* Of course it's not really all that bad to digress a little, as one is studying, as long as that digression does not cause one to lose track of the original activity. The problem is that there almost certainly won't be any links on the Cartoon Network or CNN sites that bring your students back to your oceanography site—students can literally become *lost* on the Web. You can minimize this using a few simple tricks:

1. Use the *target="blank"* addition to the HTML tag that creates a link (described earlier in this chapter). This causes the linked page to open in a new window. If a student gets lost or confused, he or she can simply close that window and your original page will be in full view.

2. Put all the links that lead to places beyond your own Web site in a special section of your site that is clearly labeled (with something like "Caution: Clicking on the links below take you to other Web sites"). Putting all the links to other sites in one spot is sometimes called creating a *link farm.*

---

*Tech Talk: Internal and External Links*

When a link takes the user to another spot within the same Web site, it is called an *internal* link. When a link takes a user to a completely different Web site, it is called an *external* link.

---

The default color for a Web link is blue: a text link is blue underlined text and a picture link has a blue border around it. It is possible to customize the link color, but we don't recommend it. Blue has become the standard link color, and sticking with the standard helps users understand the situation. And, since blue and underlined is the standard format for links, you will want to avoid making nonlinking text blue or underlined so that a user will not be tricked into thinking a link exists where it does not.

## Navigation

Links allow a user to choose his or her path through the Web. The method a person uses to find his or her way around any piece of information is called *navigation*. Each medium has its own navigational elements: a newspaper uses sections and page numbers for reference, and televisions have channel numbers. Links are an important navigational element on the Web. As you design your Web site, you will want to consider what kind of navigational support you want to build into your pages. There are basically two kinds of navigational supports on the Web: linear and nonlinear. *Linear* navigational elements help the user go through the Web pages in a specific sequence (these are often shown as *next* and *back* links). *Nonlinear* navigational elements allow a user to choose an individualized path. For example, a Web site may have links to a number of different topic areas, and these links may be visible on every page in the Web site so that a user can jump from one area to another. The same set of links appearing on each page of a site is a very common navigational support system and has its own name: *persistent navigation*. You can find examples of persistent navigation on a great many Web sites. One of the most often-copied examples of this is on the Amazon.com site (http://www.amazon.com), which uses links that are designed to look like folder tabs at the top of each page.

Persistent navigation links do not have to have fancy graphics associated with them; a simple set of links that allows the user to go to different sections of your site placed at the bottom or top of each Web page will do the job quite well.

Home | Penguin Habitats | Penguin Eating Habits
Penguins in Captivity | Links to Other Penguin Sites

**Figure 3.6**     An Example of a Persistent Navigation

> ## Common Navigation Strategies
>
> *Home*: The home page is the main page of the site. Every other page on the site contains a link that takes the user back to the main page. Often this link is an icon or picture of a house, or simply the word *home.*
>
> *Bread crumbs*: Links that typically appear near the top of a Web page in a horizontal line, listing each previous page that the user has visited to get to the current page (setting up bread crumbs requires some tricky HTML coding).
>
> *Persistent navigation:* A small set of links that appear on every page of the Web site. This might be a set of three links that simply say *back, home,* and *next,* or it might be a set of links to the main areas of a site (e.g., "about me," "homework," "class rules," "upcoming events"). These links are usually placed in the same place on every page. For example, there may be a set of links that always appear on the left side of the browser window.

## Layout

The organization of text and graphics on a page is traditionally referred to as its *layout.* When designing for a traditional display like a bulletin board or a paper handout, you have the option to place blocks or columns of text and accompanying graphics anywhere on the page that you think will look best. The Web does not allow you to do this as easily. In HTML, there is no simple way to "fix" the text and graphics in a single spot (HTML was originally designed to help scholars share drafts of their work; there was no need for any layout considerations because these were manuscripts for technical journals). HTML assumes a certain amount of fluidity in the layout of a Web page. The page can be viewed in different-sized browser windows, so the text and graphic locations automatically *wrap* themselves to fit within a browser window's horizontal dimensions. The layout will not try to fit itself into the vertical dimensions because scrolling up and down is considered a normal part of Web viewing. Therefore, when making a simple Web page, you can control the vertical layout to a large extent, but you cannot control the horizontal aspect of the layout nearly as well. The trick is to think in terms of this vertical layout without thinking too much about the horizontal layout—think in terms of designing "from top to bottom." You can use large, bold, or different-colored text to mark the beginning of new areas on a page. You can also use hard rules (the <HR> tag) to separate areas on a page.

If your information absolutely must stay together horizontally, try experimenting with *tables*. HTML has a set of tags that allow you to create tables of information. These tables can have visible dividing lines or invisible ones. Virtually any comprehensive HTML reference guide will have a great deal of information on making tables. Web editing software usually has the built-in ability to generate tables very easily. Remember though, that once you put your information into a table, the users may have to scroll horizontally to see everything if their browser window is small.

When designing a Web page, try to think of the layout as something that is constantly fluid. The text will have to wrap itself to the size the viewer's browser window. Think of placing graphic images generally instead of specifically (for example, "the picture of the penguin will go *approximately* here, with the text describing Antarctic conditions").

## SUMMARY

Web pages are created using HTML (Hypertext Markup Language). HTML is a set of format commands known as *tags*. The tags and text that comprise a Web page are called its *source code*. Among other things, tags can be used to format text and insert graphic files (it's important to keep in mind that graphics files can be displayed through a Web page, but they cannot be fully incorporated into the HTML file that comprises the Web page; they are separate files that are referenced by the HTML file). HTML is easy to create using simple word-processing software.

Web editing software can make the creation of Web pages even easier because it inserts and manages the HTML tags while displaying the page as it will look to the end user. The problem with Web editors is that they don't always insert tags correctly; good Web editing software allows editing of tags manually.

Web pages or HTML files (the two terms are synonymous) are viewed through *browser* software, which interprets the tags to put the Web page into the correct visual format. Browsers can display Web pages that are located on the same computer as the browser or they can use HTTP (Hypertext Transfer Protocol) to transfer and display Web pages that are available on remotely located computers.

A remotely located computer that is dedicated to making the files stored on it available to the public is called a *server*. Web servers are specifically dedicated to making Web page materials available. To make your own Web pages available for public display, you must have access to a Web server and you must transfer your HTML and graphics files to that server. The most common method of transferring files is FTP (File Transfer

Protocol), which can be accomplished a number of ways, including the use of free FTP software available at downloadable software database Web sites.

Web server space is sometimes available through your own school or district. Commercial server space is available through subscription to ISPs (Internet service providers) such as America Online and EarthLink. It's also possible to find free server space, but this most often comes with advertising that's inserted into your Web page's display.

Web page design and development is a three-step process that involves deciding what the site will do, what the site will look like, and actually producing the site. In the first step you decide the site's function. In the second step you decide the site's form. The first two of the three steps are accomplished using paper and pencil. Finally, in the third step you gather all the elements you are going to use for your site and actually create the HTML files.

The Web is a unique medium. People access Web pages through a wide variety of computers, browser software, and personal settings. Therefore, the best approach to Web design is to keep it simple. Using the default font (Times, 12 point) and the default format for links (blue, underlined text) is recommended.

Two important elements of Web design are *navigation* and *layout*. Navigation refers to the organization and presentation of the links used to choose a path through the Web. A *home* link and *persistent navigation* are common design strategies that help users successfully find their way around a Web site. Layout refers to the organization of text and graphics on a Web page. When designing the layout, it is important to keep in mind that, by default, Web pages adjust themselves to the size of a browser window, wrapping text and graphics to fit the horizontal dimensions of the window. A Web page's vertical layout is easier to control.

## GOING BEYOND THE CHAPTER

1. **Web Resources.**

   For obvious reasons, the Web is a great place to find support for using HTML. One of our favorite sites for HTML information is HTML Goodies (http://www.htmlgoodies.com/), an extensive site filled with tutorials and references.

   Another excellent resource is the Web Design Group's HTML Reference page (http://www.htmlhelp.com/reference/html40/). This includes an alphabetical list of all the current HTML tags.

   W3Schools.com also has a very good HTML tutorial and reference section, located at http://www.w3schools.com/html/.

2. **Reference Books.**

   A number of books delve deeply into HTML. We recommend *Learning Web Design: A Beginner's Guide to HTML, Graphics and Beyond, 2nd Edition*, by Jennifer Niederst (O'Reilly and Asssociates). Take a look at our Web site to view a listing of other reference books we recommend (http://www.drtimgreen.com/).

3. **The Webby Awards.**

   One of the best ways to improve your sense of Web design is to examine the work of successful Web designers. The International Society for Digital Arts and Sciences annually presents the *Webby Awards* for outstanding Web design (http://www.Webbyawards.com/). Visit their site and check out the Nominees and Winners section to see a variety of well-designed sites.

4. **Finding the Good in the Bad.**

   Sometimes the best way to discover what design ideas work best for you is to look at a variety of designs that do *not* work. *Vincent Flanders' Web Pages that Suck* site (http://www.webpagesthatsuck.com/) is a great collection of "problematic" Web sites. The site also has a number of resources that promote good Web design.

# Reading Between the Lines

*The Legalities and Liabilities of Using the Web in the Classroom*

## GUIDING QUESTIONS

This chapter will help you answer the following questions:

- What equity issues exist with the use of the Web in the classroom?
- What are the safety issues associated with the Web and how can I protect my students?
- What is *netiquette* and what are some basic principles?
- What is fair use?
- Can my students use copyrighted material in their multimedia projects?

## KEY TERMS

Acceptable Use Policy

Copyright

Digital divide

Fair Use

Filtering software

Netiquette

## OVERVIEW

Throughout this book we discuss and show examples of how using the Web in the classroom can provide positive learning opportunities for your students. Despite the benefits, there are common pitfalls and issues you should understand that are associated with using the Web in the classroom. Thus, the intent of this chapter is to move beyond the design and development of Web projects to examine issues that inevitably arise as the use of the Web is integrated into teaching and learning. The following sections provide you with an overview of the liabilities and legalities associated with the use of the Internet and Web that promote responsible and healthy applications of Web use.

It begins with an overview of issues that surround equity of access to computing technologies, referred to as the *digital divide,* and covers such topics as socioeconomic status, gender, and accessibility for students with disabilities. Student safety and the use of the Web is a huge concern in schools, and we provide suggestions and resources for protecting students from inappropriate content and strangers. This includes brief descriptions of commonly used online communication tools, a review of common concerns, and suggestions for establishing classroom rules. Guidelines for being a responsible user of the Web are provided, which includes examples of proper computer etiquette, or *netiquette.* Finally, we end with an overview of the legal expectations associated with the use of Web content in the development of classroom Web projects.

## ISSUES OF EQUITY

As we've mentioned in previous chapters, the use of the Internet and the Web has become common throughout the United States and the world. It has changed how we do business, it has changed education, and it has changed society in general. When digital technologies became more available for both home and school use, a noticeable discrepancy developed between various groups within society. The term *digital divide* was coined to describe those who could actually afford access to a computer and an Internet connection and those who could not. Over the last decade, as the cost of computing technology has dropped, the gap between the "haves" and "have nots" has decreased, but a gap still remains.

More recently, the definition of digital divide has grown from an "either/or" to include the idea of quality. There are differences in the quality of technology available, and differences in how technology is used in homes, schools, and communities. Although some digital equity issues have been addressed, many facets of the digital divide need to be resolved—issues relative to ethnicity, socioeconomics, and gender. We believe that as educators, our choices about the use of technology can influence and help to negate the impact of the digital divide.

## Ethnicity and Socioeconomic Issues

When we encourage and support the use of the Web and other digital technologies in our classroom, making informed decisions may actually decrease the digital divide. This starts with first recognizing those issues and situations that are symptomatic of inequities. Those who are at a disadvantage are the least likely to have access to technological hardware and software. This includes those from poor families, high poverty areas, and minority populations. As income levels increase across ethnic groups, so does technology use. Recent surveys have shown that certain groups are more likely to have access to technology. For example, Caucasian and Asian students are twice as likely to access and utilize technology than are students from other ethnic groups (National Telecommunications and Information Administration, 2000).

Access to technology within the schools, however, does not guarantee that use is equitable among ethnic and cultural groups. Schools located in high poverty areas that do have technology are more likely to use computing technology for drill and practice activities. This differs from schools in more affluent areas, where students are more likely to use technology in constructivist activities, such as engaging in problem solving and projects that encourage higher-level thinking. Given this divide, we need to make sure that students who are asked to complete technology-based projects outside of school actually have access to the necessary tools, and that methods that we select within our classrooms actually encourage the development of higher-order thinking, regardless of socioeconomic status, ethnic or cultural affiliations, and community.

## Gender

Just as there has been a discrepancy in the number of women entering math and science careers, females are underrepresented among information technology professionals; only 20 percent are women. However, more women than men spend time online. When we preview books for our classroom, we make sure to include books and texts that are free of stereotypes and gender bias. We also make sure that books and texts appeal to the female students in our classroom. These same criteria should be applied to any Web sites and software that we use in teaching. Any content that we use or create needs to be screened for bias.

Even though none of us intentionally practices gender bias, it exists throughout the Web and it likely exists within our schools. To reduce gender bias we must first maintain high standards for *all* students. Within the classroom, both male and female students should be given equal opportunities for leadership roles in technology projects. This can be supported in part through the use of best practices in cooperative learning and grouping when designing Web-based learning activities, which can help foster positive social interactions and create positive learning environments. Such learning environments are more inclusive and less likely to reinforce inequities.

*Curriculum Resource: Web Site.* For more information on how to prevent gender bias, you may consider visiting The National Coalition for Women and Girls in Education Web site at http://www.ncwge .org. The publication *Title IX at 30: Report Card on Gender Equity* is available through this site and provides an overview of gender equity in several areas, including technology.

## Disabilities

In 1998, Congress amended the Rehabilitation Act, requiring federally funded agencies to make Web sites and other electronic information accessible to people with disabilities. The law, called Section 508 (29 USC '794d), requires that persons with disabilities have access to the same public information that is available to persons without disabilities. Although the legally required level of accessibility has recently come into question, making all projects accessible to persons with disabilities and creating digital learning opportunities for students with disabilities is simply good inclusive practice. We recommend considering two aspects of accessibility when developing multimedia projects and when integrating the use of the Web into class content: helping students with disabilities access the Web, and making your own Web sites accessible to students with disabilities.

### Accessing the World Wide Web

Many digital advances have made it possible for people with a wide array of challenges to access information on the Web. These technologies are often referred to as *assistive technologies*. This includes the use of hardware, such as specially designed mice and keyboards, for those whose physical challenges make traditional input devices difficult to use. Other assistive technologies, such as screen readers, can read aloud any text that appears on the screen. Although assistive technologies for accessing the Web are beyond the scope of this text, they are surprisingly affordable and readily available (Bray, Brown, & Green, 2004). By utilizing the array of available assistive technologies, virtually any person, regardless of disability, can interact with the Web. It's often a matter of knowing where to look for the available technologies. Your special education teacher or school psychologist may be able to assist you in locating appropriate technologies for particular students.

### Creating Accessible Multimedia Projects

An accessible Web Site is one that's compatible with multiple assistive technologies and easily accessed by persons with disabilities. For example, when a picture is labeled with alternate text, the use of a screen reader will allow a person with a visual impairment to hear that text read aloud in order to hear a version of what others see on the screen. To ensure that a Web site makes use of these accessibility features, numerous organizations and companies offer pay-for-service and free accessibility checks of Web sites. One commonly used service, called *Bobby* (http://webxact .watchfire.com/), will conduct a free evaluation of Web material. This service will tell how user-friendly a site is when being accessed by common assistive technologies. Most hardware and computer programs will explicitly state what types of technology devices they support or are compatible with.

---

*Curriculum Integration Idea:*
*Web Accessibility Web Sites*

Programs such as Microsoft Office include built-in accessibility features. The screen can be enlarged through a magnifier tool and the colors can be adjusted for individuals with visual impairments. Office also includes limited text to speech capabilities, as well as voice recognition.

## STUDENT SAFETY

Students grow up with computers. Over 96 percent of kids under the age of 15 have reported spending time on the Internet (USC, 2004). Surfing the Web, IM, and sending e-mails are common forms of communication between kids of all ages. Although these interactive activities have many benefits, they also have perils. As we increase the use of the Internet in our classroom and encourage interactivity through Web-based projects, it's important to teach our students about safety and simultaneously make sure we are protecting our students. Accessing and viewing inappropriate sites and communicating with strangers are two key safety issues that teachers must teach students to properly handle.

## Protecting Students From Inappropriate Content

Federal legislation makes it a requirement that all school districts adopt policies to prevent students from accessing inappropriate material. Before you begin Web projects, it's important to check out your district's policy on the use of the Web. Most districts will have an *acceptable use policy (AUP)*, which outlines expectations for staff and for students. These written guidelines generally require a signature of agreement.

> ### The Consortium for School Networking
>
> The Consortium for School Networking provides an overview of the Children's Internet Protection Act. This legislation made it a requirement that schools adopt policies to protect students from inappropriate content on the Internet if they wanted to receive federal funding for educational technology. You may visit this site at http://cosn.org/.

Anyone who has surfed the Web knows that it's easy to accidentally find yourself on an inappropriate Web page. To combat this problem, most school districts have purchased *filtering software*, which attempts to screen out those undesirable sites. The downside is that such software often inadvertently restricts access to sites that are educationally appropriate. If your district has filtering software in place and you cannot access desired sites, it's usually a simple matter of letting the person in charge of technology know what sites you are being blocked from. She or he can then make an administrative adjustment to the filter to make the requested sites available.

### Filtering Software Examples

No filtering software is 100 percent effective. Even if you have filtering software, it's still possible for students to have access to less than desirable sites, including blogs, wikis, and social spaces. This can happen for several reasons, but it most often happens because the developers of some sites want to bypass filtering software. Unfortunately, we still have individuals and groups who intentionally make Web sites that are designed to get by filters. Such sites are often called *malicious sites*. Groups who create malicious sites often have a political agenda and may specifically target children with the intent to spread misinformation; this is done by masquerading as an educational or informational Web site. Because of this, we must carefully screen those sites that our students use or include in Web projects. Many hoax or fictitious sites promote fake products or places and intentionally provide misinformation. For a concise overview and examples of the types of misinformation, see the September 2000 issue of the *Searcher* at http://www.infotoday.com/searcher/sep00/piper.htm (Piper, 2000).

Directly teaching students how to evaluate a Web site for content and accuracy will go a long way in preventing problems with misinformation. As for inappropriate content, your classroom *computer use agreement* should explicitly state how students should proceed when they encounter an inappropriate site and state the consequences for intentionally accessing such sites. It is usually a good idea to have students immediately notify the teacher upon accessing an inappropriate site.

## Protecting Students From Strangers

Besides surfing the Internet, students spend time interacting with others through many of the available Web communication systems. As teachers, we need to make sure that students (and parents) are aware of risks and hazards associated with various types of online engagement. We must then establish ground rules for home and the classroom, and educate students on the hazards of both communicating with strangers and making personal information public. Because most online communication is text based, it's easy for a person to pretend to be someone that he or she is not. Unhealthy adults have been known to masquerade as children or teenagers. The following section provides concerns associated with a variety of commonly used communication tools.

### E-mail

This is the tool that most all of us are very familiar with. Students can have personal e-mail accounts and send messages back and forth to others.

**Concern:** E-mail is often a targeted for spam or other inappropriate and unsolicited advertisements. It's not always possible to verify who you are actually communicating with.

### Instant Messaging

Students chat with friends through IM programs. These programs allow students to communicate in real time with other individuals that are on their "buddy" lists.

> **Concern:** To participate in IM, the user usually has to provide a profile of personal information. Also, people can falsify information and present themselves as something other than their true selves (for example, a child may not be honest about his or her age and begin engaging in conversations with adults, or an adult may masquerade as a young boy or girl). Parents (and teachers) should check students' "buddies." Many of the online accounts, like Yahoo!, have parental controls that allow the parent or adult access to a child's friend list.

### Chat Rooms

Chat rooms allow for conversations to occur in real time and are generally centered around a topic of interest. You have to join a chat room, and membership can be available to anyone or through invitation only. Dialogue then proceeds in either a public or private forum.

> **Concern:** As with IM, participants usually need to provide a profile with which it is easy to give out identifiable information. Most chat rooms are unmonitored for content and language. An additional caution is that participants in a chat room can request inappropriate content, such as pictures, from other members and have it directly e-mailed to the requesting party.

### Groups

Many online services allow users to form private groups where only certain people are allowed to join. A moderator makes choices as to who is allowed to participate in the online community. As a teacher (or parent), you can choose to be a moderator. This is a great way for you to control who is communicating with the students.

> **Concern:** You may not know what groups your students are participating in and you may not be granted access to groups that your student belongs to. If you're not allowed to view the group, then it is safe to assume that the moderator has ill intent and the group is not appropriate. If you are invited to join a group, and you do not personally know each member, there is always a potential risk.

### Message Boards/Discussion Boards

These forums allow individuals to post messages or responses to discussions or topics. They are very public. Participants can often post pictures and respond to each other's comments.

> **Concern:** As with all Web communication, personal information may be accessible to anyone. Under no circumstances should students divulge any personal information, including full names, telephone numbers, or addresses. If the message board is in a public forum, it's not always possible to monitor content.

### Blogs

As mentioned in Chapter 1, *blog* is short for *Web log*, which started out as online diaries and are now used in a variety of ways. There are individual blogs in which a person posts content and others are allowed to read and respond. The writer of the blog can choose who is allowed to respond. Other blogs have been set up to operate similar to discussion boards, allowing people to post messages and respond to each other in a public forum.

> **Concern:** Many blogs contain adult content and should be screened. Just like discussion boards, you won't always know who is participating. Blog content is frequently unmonitored. Also, students who maintain blogs may not fully realize the public nature of the Web—it's always safest to assume that all information posted on the Web becomes public information, but a great many young people presume the information that they post is accessible only to friends.

### Personal Web Pages and Classroom Web Pages

Web Pages are a great way for students and teachers to share information. They are commonplace in school districts and schools. They are also a popular way of sharing information.

> **Concern:** Placing any identifying information—pictures, school, phone numbers, or addresses—means that anyone with Web access can see this information. Some parents may not want to have their child's picture, or any identifying information, made public. Most districts and schools require written consent from parents before making pictures, names, and student work visible online. Even so, it is generally a good idea to use first names only and to avoid the use of any information that may make it possible for a stranger to identify a student or his or her home. A rule of

thumb adopted by many schools is that either a child's picture or a child's name may be posted on a Web page, but never both.

Online groups, discussion boards, e-mail, and personal blogs and Web pages create exciting educational media that can increase learning through communication. Conscious planning and informed supervision will go a long way in keeping students safe while on the Web.

## Establishing Ground Rules for Your Classroom

Students are particularly trusting of information that they find on the Web and are susceptible to predators. If you are using the Web in your classroom, it is your responsibility to have measures in place to protect students. This includes not only supervising students, but establishing and explicitly teaching guidelines and ground rules. Rules for student Internet use and communication should be clearly written and posted. Prior to use of the Web, you should discuss the rationale for each of the rules with your classroom. The following rules are recommended by the USC Annenberg School Center for the Digital Future (2004).

- If a conversation makes you uncomfortable, leave the discussion and report it to your teacher.
- Do not respond to rude or threatening messages.
- Always use kind language. Avoid flaming. (Flaming is explained in the next section).
- Do not share any personal information including your name, age, school, or where you live.

Many classroom teachers will send home a permission slip for use of the Internet and the Web with a copy of class rules and guidelines. We also recommend inviting parents in for an open house to share information as to how they may keep their children safe at home. Many parents are truly unaware of the types of communication tools available and what types of sites their kids are visiting.

> You may wish to investigate the use of your browser's history tool. This is found in "Internet Options" and on most browsers. You can set it to keep track of the Web sites visited by users of your computer for several days.

## NETIQUETTE

As we grow up, the adults in our lives teach us the rules of proper behavior in different social situations. What is proper in one setting may not be proper in another. When we go to visit Aunt Mary, we learn from a very early age to put our napkins in our laps, use the correct fork for our salad, and always say please and thank you. When asking our mom why we have to follow these rules, she says that this is simply proper "etiquette" at Aunt Mary's house. Just as rules define appropriate social behavior in various social settings, rules also define appropriate social behavior on the Web. This is called *netiquette.*

### Being a Responsible User of the Web

A story about two different viewpoints (this really happened to one of us!):

> A few weeks ago I was having dinner with a friend at a small restaurant. The waitress provided excellent service by keeping our water glasses full and making sure we had everything that we needed. When we had finished eating, she promptly brought the check and approached the table a few times during our post dinner conversation to ask if we wanted anything else. After returning a second time to offer more coffee, my friend nearly exploded, "I can't believe American waitresses! They are always rushing you out the door so they can get your money!" I was thoroughly surprised by his response to what I perceived as excellent service. He continued, "In my country the wait people never pester you at the end of the meal. They let you enjoy your conversation and are patient enough to wait until you ask for the check!" I couldn't help but smile. "Interesting," I responded. "When I was in your country last summer I was really frustrated by having to ask for my check. I thought that the wait people were horribly rude and simply not bringing me the check because they wanted me to spend more money!"

Just as customs and social rules vary from country to country, social rules vary in different places on the Web. What is appropriate in one venue may not be acceptable in another. And, just as it's important for world travelers to understand and follow the accepted social rules in countries other than their own, it is important for users of the Web to have a firm understanding of what is socially appropriate online. Netiquette is something that students need to be taught and something that students (and adults) should practice. The Web is a highly interactive and social place. The following section briefly outlines responsibilities of the personal user of the Web and provides a few guiding principles for participation in differing Web forums.

### Guidelines

The Internet has become a major tool of communication. Through e-mail we interact with friends, family, and other professionals. As discussed in the previous section, we also communicate through groups, discussion boards, and blogs. We even communicate through the development of Web pages and Web sites. Because digital communication is highly text based, a new symbol system has developed to help communicate voice inflection, emotion, and writer's intent. Each of these forms of written and interactive communication requires an understanding of these new words, acronyms, and symbols that are meant to facilitate communication.

Another true story:

> Recently a colleague asked a question concerning my thoughts about the professionalism displayed by an acquaintance who sent an e-mail to a small group of people. When I asked what had bothered her she said, "I am just not sure what to think about someone who has so much love." Puzzled I asked her what she was referring to. She said, "She kept writing 'LOL' in her e-mail and I am not sure what 'Lots of Love' has to do with anything." LOL, when used in e-mail, stands for "laughing out loud," which is meant to help communicate that what was written is to be interpreted as funny. My colleague wasn't aware of the meaning of the acronym and consequently had been upset.

To minimize miscommunication, it is helpful to understand the short cuts that have been created in an attempt to communicate an author's intent. Even though these shortcuts and symbols were developed to facilitate meaning (or to decrease the amount of key strokes) being uninformed or using them with others who do not understand them can create confusion. To avoid the pitfalls described we recommend that you first familiarize yourself with emoticons, acronyms, and symbols that are commonly used in online communication.

### Emoticons

The word *emoticon* is a combination of two words: *emotion* and *icon*. Using the Internet for communication can be problematic, as it can be difficult to communicate in text exactly what we mean or how we feel. When we talk we use voice inflection, facial expression, and body language. This isn't possible through the Web (unless you are connected to a Webcam)! Emoticons are used to help communicate meaning within text and are generally symbols of facial expressions created through a combination of keystrokes. When the keystrokes are entered, some computer programs will convert the emoticon into an icon. Some common emoticons are:

```
:-)        = happy or smile

:-(        = sad

>:-(       = beyond sad, angry!

:-/        = skeptical
```

Students who participate in IM and in online groups often have an extensive emoticon vocabulary!

### Acronyms

The use of acronyms developed in chat rooms as real-time conversations began to take place, and they are used as a form of shorthand communication. A few common ones are:

```
LOL        = Laughing out loud

ROFL       = Rolling on the floor, laughing

BTW        = By the way

AFK        = Away from keyboard

PDS        = Please don't shout (when typing
             messages online, using all capital
             letters is considered the equiva-
             lent of shouting)

F2F        = Face to face

TTYL       = Talk to you later
```

Acronyms can easily be misinterpreted and it's difficult for most of us to keep up on the new ones that seem to be created daily! Generally acronyms, like emoticons, are best suited to chat rooms and communication with personal acquaintances who are willing to ask us for clarification if we confuse them or provide us with clarification if we are confused.

### Flaming

Flaming refers to online derogatory or insulting comments and general personal attacks. Flaming can happen when one person becomes angry and posts a message without thoroughly thinking through his or her response. Or, flaming can simply occur when someone is just plain rude! (Sad, but true.) Careful thought and planning can help to eliminate flames. It's completely acceptable to use emoticons or other types of expressive symbols when trying to avoid misinterpretation of your message. Before posting an angry response, ask for clarification. Keep in mind that it's much easier to attack a person online than it is face to face, and there is a tendency for the offended party to flame back. Students need to be taught to refrain from flaming and how to handle a flame. Online bullies can be just as detrimental as playground bullies, and their participation in an online venue is sure to halt communication.

### Additional Guidelines

Proper netiquette for the use of e-mail, chat rooms, and discussion boards will vary depending on each one's purpose. Just as we have traditionally taught the differences between writing a letter to a friend and writing a business letter, there are key differences in what is acceptable in various online situations. Here are a few initial suggestions.

- When communicating professionally or formally, avoid the use of jargon, acronyms, and emoticons. A business e-mail should be written with the same care that one would write a business letter. When embarking on Web projects that involve communication with other classrooms and schools, local businesses, adults, or community members, one should employ a more "formal" tone.
- The use of fancy backgrounds and fonts should be avoided with formal communication. Even in informal communication, this can be annoying as it can slow the loading of a page or e-mail message.
- Never use all caps. This is considered rude and a form of digital yelling in all communication venues.
- In friendship or personal e-mails, using chat language, including emoticons and acronyms, is fine. However, don't assume that everyone knows all of the chat language.
- Break large sections of text into paragraphs.
- Forwarding chain letters is generally considered rude.

Finally, it's important to remember that as the teacher you are responsible for both what your students post and what they view. You will want to review student work prior to making it public, as well as to keep up on the types of Web sites that are being accessed.

## FAIR USE GUIDELINES

So far this chapter has discussed the liabilities, or concerns, of Web use. Most of the issues focused on student use of the Web for communication or the purpose of accessing information. These activities are often precursors to creating your own Web projects. This section discusses the legalities of using what is found on the Web: text, pictures, video, and sound.

### Copyright

Basically, according to copyright law, any material—written work, pictures, sound, and movies—that you do not create is considered the property of someone else (usually either the work's creator or the organization for whom it was created). To use another person's material, you must have permission. If you fail to ask permission, you are breaking the law. The Web has made it very easy to access information and resources, especially for use in multimedia projects. In simple terms, it is easy to steal. However, guidelines can be followed that allow students and teachers to use portions of copyrighted material in multimedia presentations, as long as the presentations are for noncommercial, educational purposes. These are referred to as the guidelines of *fair use.*

There are four factors to consider when determining whether one can use copyrighted material. Just because your purpose is educational, doesn't mean that it's okay to use anything you find. The factors are:

1. The purpose of the multimedia project (Is it commercial or for nonprofit educational purposes?)

2. The nature of the copyrighted material

3. The amount or percentage of the portion used

4. The effect of the use on the potential market for, or value of, the copyrighted work

### Guidelines

Truly understanding fair use is a complex process. The fair use guidelines are designed to help judges make a decision if a copyright infringement suit is brought to court, and ultimately it is a court that decides if copyright law has been violated. However, you and your students can follow some guidelines when incorporating material into your multimedia project to limit any legal implications. The following are general rules for determining how much of a specific medium is considered fair to use without first obtaining permission from the copyright holder.

- *Motion media.* Up to 10 percent or three minutes, whichever is less.
- *Text.* 10 percent or 1,000 words, whichever is less.
- *Poems.* An entire poem up to 250 words may be used, but no more than three poems by one poet or five poems by different poets from any anthology. For longer poems, 250 words may be used.
- *Music, lyrics, and music video.* Up to 10 percent but no more than 30 seconds. Any alterations shall not change the basic melody or the character of the work.
- *Illustrations and photographs.* No more than five images by an artist or a photographer.
- *Numerical data sets.* Up to 10 percent or 2,500 cell entries, whichever is less.

Written permission from the copyright holder is required when:

- The multimedia project is distributed for commercial reproduction or distribution.
- Your multimedia project can be viewed over an electronic network (this is considered public distribution).

When using media that you have not personally created, always acknowledge the owners of the work. Credit must be given where credit is due. If you used copyrighted material, even legally, you need to provide the ownership information. This includes a full bibliographic description (author, title, publisher, date, and place of publication), and it must be listed in a credit or bibliography section.

Fair use guidelines are intended to allow educators to make use of portions of copyrighted material for educational purposes under the assumption that the work is to be used in limited capacity (for example, used in your own classroom) and for a limited time. The "limited time" consideration allows educators to make use of portions of copyrighted work immediately to support an educational objective without having to wait days, weeks, or months to receive permission from the owner. If you are going to continually use a copyrighted work (for example, a song, a picture, or a poem) over the course of multiple years or semesters, it is your responsibility to obtain copyright permission.

## Commercial Content

Finally, before you embark on the development of multimedia projects and the use of the Internet in your classroom, you will want to consciously make a decision about the amount of commercial content that you will allow into your classroom. Many of the free online Web tools remain free because they include advertisements. We suggest that you ask yourself some of the following questions before utilizing any Web sites or tools with advertisements: Who is the sponsor of the commercial content? Is their product healthy for kids? Does the product encourage positive interpersonal interactions and promote social responsibility? How distracting is the commercial content? Ultimately, you have to make the decision as to the cost benefit of using any Web-based tools that contain commercial content.

## SUMMARY

Successful and safe use of the Web requires an understanding of the legalities and liabilities associated with the use of public networks and multimedia in the classroom. Even though access to the Web has grown tremendously, a digital divide remains. Differences in how the Web is used and access to quality digital tools varies between genders and among ethnic groups, and is influenced by socioeconomic status. The divide can be mitigated through conscious choices made by teachers who are implementing Web projects. Access to the Web can be increased for persons with disabilities through the use of assistive technologies and by creating more accessible Web sites.

Student safety is a primary concern when using the Web. Web-based communication tools, such as e-mail, IM, chat rooms, blogs, groups, and discussion boards, all contain risks as well as benefits. The risks can be minimized through the implementation and enforcement of acceptable use policies and through the use of tools such as filtering software. However, teacher awareness and direct instruction on appropriate and inappropriate uses and hazards, as well as clear home and classroom ground rules, are equally if not more important and will go a long way in keeping students safe.

Being a responsible user of the Web also requires an understanding of netiquette, which is simply polite behavior online. Netiquette rules vary depending on the purpose or use of the Web, and understanding the meanings of basic emoticons and acronyms, as well as when and when not to use them, increases the likelihood that appropriate netiquette is being used.

Finally, both students and teachers need to be aware of copyright law and fair use guidelines. Fair use guidelines help you to determine when and how much copyrighted material can be used in an educational project.

The purpose of this chapter was to provide you with a foundation to help you plan and use Web projects that considers issues of equity and protects students from strangers and inappropriate content. Familiarizing yourself with these ideas will protect not only your students, but you as well, from accusations of misconduct. No system or plan is 100 percent fail safe, and it's up to us, the teachers, to inform ourselves and parents as to the types of activities that our students participate in.

## GOING BEYOND THE CHAPTER

1. **Analyzing Web Site Content.**

   To demonstrate to students how easy it is to be fooled by information on a Web site, you may want to consider an activity where a hoax Web site and a credible Web site are compared. For example, divide students into groups and have them "research" the city Mankato, Minnesota. Provide each group with the same set of research questions that includes basic information such as annual temperature, colleges, sites of interest, and location. Provide half of the class with a link to a hoax city of Mankato Web site (http://city-mankato .us/), and the other group uses the actual Mankato, Minnesota, Web site (http://www.ci.mankato.mn.us/). Compare findings. Engage the class in a follow-up discussion on how to make sure that the information that one is reading is accurate.

2. **Parent Involvement.**

   Get parents involved in monitoring online use. Have an evening workshop and introduce parents to the types of online communication and activities that their children may be involved in and help them create home Internet use agreements. A great resource for organizing an event (or for sharing with parents), called NetSafeKids: A Resource for Concerned Parents, can be found online at http://www.nap.edu/netsafe kids/index.html

3. **Acceptable Use Policies.**

   Most, if not all, school districts and schools have developed acceptable use policies that outline the expectations of student use of technology at school. Take the time to find out what guidelines your school district and school have regarding student use of technology. If you are familiar with the guidelines, review them to see how comprehensive they are and what your student must follow. You can also do a search on the Web through Google (http://www.google.com/) using the term *acceptable use policy* to read examples of what school districts have created.

# Resource A

# The Basics of the Internet and the Web

## *A Refresher*

**S**everal of the concepts and ideas provided that follow can be found in other parts of the book. Despite this, we have included this information here in case you need a basic refresher on the Internet and the Web. This information could also be used to share with your students to provide them with a foundation of the Internet and Web. We begin by describing what the Web is and its relationship with the Internet. We include a brief history of the Web by discussing who developed it and why (a slightly expanded version of what you can find in Chapter 1). The chapter concludes with a discussion of its current state and where experts believe it might be headed.

### WHAT IS THE WEB?

To understand what the Web is, we need to take a step back and first discuss a larger concept. This concept is the *Internet*. Because the Web is part of the Internet, understanding what the Internet is and how it works will help you tackle the concept of the Web.

So, what is the Internet? The Internet is a worldwide collection of *computer networks* that allows individuals to share data from one computer to another. This collection of computer networks is made up of various types of specific computers or groups of computers that are located at places such as schools, businesses, and the government. In essence, the Internet is a network of networks.

These computer networks transmit data through various media—the most typical are telephone lines, coaxial cable, fiber-optic cable lines, and satellites. The data generally is not transmitted directly from one specific computer network to another; data is typically passed along through a series of intermediaries (other computer networks) that take the data from its starting point to its intended destination. So, if you were to send data using your classroom computer (which is connected to your school's computer network) to a friend's computer (which is connected to his school's computer network) located in a classroom in a different town, the data would be transferred several times through different computer networks before it finally reached your friend's computer.

### The "Language" of the Internet

To transmit data from one computer to another, as we've been discussing, specific agreed upon protocols need to be used. The major protocol is called *Transmission Control Protocol/Internet Protocol (TCP/IP)*. This protocol was developed to allow different types of computers (such as Apple, IBM, Linux, Sun) to connect to each other (in other words, "speak" to each other; this is referred to as *handshaking*). Most, if not all computers, come with a version of TCP/IP software and therefore have the capacity to transmit data over the Internet.

---

### LAN and WAN

Two terms you will hear in conjunction with computer networks are *LAN* and *WAN*. LAN stands for local area network. A LAN is a small group of computers connected together with the ability to share data over a limited physical area. An example is a law office consisting of a paralegal, two lawyers, and three secretaries, where each person has his or her own computer that can share data throughout the office. A WAN, or wide area network, refers to a much larger group of computers connected together with the ability to share data over a larger physical area. A university's computer system is often considered a wide area network. A WAN is typically made up of a series of LANS all connected together.

---

## A Comparison: The Internet and the U.S. Postal Service

The structure of the Internet can be thought of in terms of the United States Postal Service (USPS). Both the Internet and the USPS are in the business of making sure that data is passed along from one location to another. The USPS is made up of various local post offices that serve different communities. These local post offices are connected to larger post offices, which are part of larger regions. These regions make up the entire United States. In addition to delivering mail within the United States, the USPS can deliver mail to countries around the world. Once the mail is delivered to a foreign country, that country's mail structure takes over to deliver the mail (most work in roughly the same fashion, but maybe not as efficiently).

This arrangement is much like how the Internet is structured, in that it is made up of a collection of smaller computer networks, which are connected to larger computer networks that make up a worldwide computer network. Data goes from your computer through various computer networks until the data is eventually delivered to its intended location.

In addition to structure, other similarities can be found in how e-mail is sent via the Internet and how the USPS functions. Let's consider how a letter gets delivered from your house to your cousin's house. Say you live in Southern California—La Habra to be exact—and you have written a letter to your cousin in Dowagiac, Michigan. How would that letter get to your cousin if you sent it through the USPS? After writing the letter, you'd place it in an envelope and seal it. You'd place the appropriate stamp on the letter along with your address and the address of your cousin. You'd place the letter in your mailbox and it would sit there until your mail carrier picked up the letter. The letter would then travel to your local post office, where it would be sorted according to the ZIP code. The letter then would be routed to a larger post office—most likely in Long Beach or Los Angeles. Once at the larger post office, it would be placed with other letters that were headed to the same location or a similar location. The letters would travel either by plane or truck to a regional post office located in a large urban area—probably Grand Rapids, Michigan, or maybe Chicago. The letter will get sorted at this post office to be delivered to a smaller post office in Dowagiac. The letter will again be sorted based on a specific route taken by a mail carrier who delivers directly to your cousin's house. The mail carrier will drop off the letter at the house, where your cousin will have access to it.

## Internet Resources

Different resources utilize the Internet to allow you to manipulate and send data. Each resource has its own unique characteristics, but the common purpose is always communication—the sending and receiving of data from one computer to another. The two most common *Internet resources* are e-mail, and, of course, the Web. Let's briefly talk about each and how they work.

### E-mail

Unless you are a total newcomer to the Internet or have just recently been rescued from a deserted island where you were stranded for the past 25 years, you have probably used e-mail (electronic mail). The major purpose of e-mail is to allow you to exchange text messages with another individual. This was actually the original purpose for the Internet as well.

A basic e-mail software package includes a text editor that allows you to compose messages. The messages you compose can be sent directly to another person through the Internet, assuming you know that person's e-mail address. An e-mail address (see Figure A.1) identifies the location where the message you composed is to be sent. This location corresponds to an *e-mail server* that has a physical location somewhere in the world, and is connected to the Internet through a computer network. When you send your message, it is transmitted from your computer through the Internet to the e-mail server where the person you sent the message to has a mailbox (personal storage space, which is located on the e-mail server). The message you send will remain in the person's mailbox until he or she accesses it from his or her computer.

### The Web

The World Wide Web—or the *Web* as it is commonly called—is another Internet resource that allows you to access data over the Internet. The data that can be accessed on the Web is developed into documents called

tgreen@exchange.fullerton.edu

1 = the username/user ID
2 = the location of where the e-mail will be sent
3 = the type of e-mail provider

This account is for Tim Green who works at California State University, Fullerton.

**Figure A.1**    Dissection of an E-mail Address

*Web pages,* which can include text, images, audio, video, and *hyperlinks.* Hyperlinks allow you to move to and from Web pages.

For you to access a Web page and view its contents, a *browser,* such as Netscape Navigator or Microsoft Internet Explorer, needs to be used. A browser's main function is to take the content of a Web page, translate it, and then properly display it on your computer screen. A browser does this by interpreting the language that a Web page is created in, which in most instances is *hypertext markup language (HTML).* We won't spend time discussing HTML in detail here because you can read all about HTML in Chapter 3 as you learn to create your own Web page!

For your browser to display the contents of a Web page, you must know the specific location of that page; you need to know where the page resides in the network of computers that makes up the Internet, and then feed this information to your browser by typing in the location. This location is called a *Web address* (see Figure A.2) or a *universal resource locater (URL),* as it is technically called.

The Web address corresponds to a specific *Web server* (much like an e-mail server that we discussed previously) that has a physical location somewhere in the world, and is connected to the Internet. A Web server will house the Web page that you want to access. When you type in the Web address in your browser, a specific Internet protocol is used—*hypertext transfer protocol (HTTP).* HTTP has two main functions: locating and retrieving. HTTP works by going through the Internet and locating the Web page you asked your browser to find. If the page actually exists, then

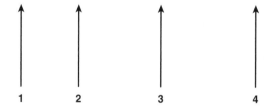

http://anacostia.si.edu/Lecture_Files/Lectures_Navitation.htm

1   2   3   4

1 = *The protocol.* The most typical protocol used on the Web is http. You may also see https, which indicates a secure Web site that is normally used to send and receive sensitive information such as credit card information.

2 = *The domain.* The name of the computer (Web server) where the Web site is located.

3 = *The directory.* The exact location on the computer (Web server) where you are trying to access.

4 = *The file.* The exact Web page file you are trying to display.

**Figure A.2**     The Anatomy of a Web Address

the contents of the Web page will be retrieved from the Web server and be given to your browser. Once your browser has the Web page contents, it then will interpret the content and display it on your computer screen. If your Web browser cannot locate a Web page from the URL you typed into the browser, an error message will be displayed on your computer screen indicating that the page could not be found.

---

### Are the Internet and the Web the Same Thing?

You will often hear people use the words *Internet* and the *Web* interchangeably. Are the Internet and the Web the same thing? This is a tricky question. We aren't trying to trick you by posing this question; however, we do want you to know the answer for it. If you have read through the previous parts of this book, you will know the answer. The envelope please—and the answer is: no, the Internet and the Web are not one in the same.

---

## HOW CAN YOU ACCESS THE WEB?

We have discussed what the Web is and how we go about displaying Web pages that are located on the Web. What we haven't discussed is how you can actually gain access to the Web. In the simplest of terms, you need a computer, a browser, and a connection to the Internet for access to the Web. The connection to the Internet is typically facilitated through an *internet service provider (ISP)*. An ISP provides individuals (and organizations) with access to the Internet by allowing an individual to connect a computer to the ISP's computer network, and use the medium in which the ISP transmits data. Is there a catch to this? Well, sort of. A fee is involved—typically a monthly one—that often ranges from $10 to $60. Once you have a connection to the Internet, you can access the Web.

Most schools provide their staffs with Web access at school. Schools can provide this because they have secured a connection to the Internet for their entire school's computer network through an ISP. The school, of course, pays for this access.

## WHO OWNS THE INTERNET AND THE WEB?

It stands to reason that if you pay to access the Internet in order to get to the Web, then someone or some group must own the Web. Well, this isn't the case. No one person or group officially owns the Internet—and therefore, this also holds true for the Web. What is owned are the mediums by which the data is transmitted—such as telephone lines, fiber-optic cable lines, and satellites. Various corporations, universities, and the government own these mediums and lease or rent access to them.

Let's say you pay $50 a month to your local cable company (which would be considered your ISP) to have a connection to the Internet to access the Web. The money you are paying technically provides you with access to use their cable lines, in essence, to send and retrieve data from different computer networks all over the world (remember, that's what the Internet is all about—transmitting data from one computer to another). So, for the $50 a month, you can connect to the Internet and use various Internet resources like e-mail and the Web. Your cable company agrees to make sure they keep their cable lines working properly so you always have access to the Internet.

---

### Bandwidth

Bandwidth refers to the amount of data that can be transferred through a digital connection in a given time period. Why should you be concerned with bandwidth? Let's explore this. When you log on to the Internet through your ISP to access the Web, the amount of time it takes for the Web pages you are accessing to appear (referred to as *download*) is due to the amount of bandwidth you have available. The better your connection to the Internet, the more bandwidth you will have available and the faster your Web pages will download to your computer screen. For example, if you access the Internet through a dial-up connection (i.e., your telephone line), your bandwidth is less than if you accessed the Internet through a cable connection. Web pages that have audio, video, or high-quality images require a high level of bandwidth to access.

Cable or DSL (digital subscriber line) are referred to as *broadband* Internet connections because they allow multiple pieces of data to be sent at one time; thus, speeding up the time it takes to access and send data over the Internet. A dial-up connection is not considered to be broadband.

---

## A BRIEF HISTORY OF THE WORLD WIDE WEB: THE WHO, WHAT, WHEN, AND WHY

As discussed in Chapter 1, the concept of what has become the Web is credited to Tim Berners-Lee while he was a researcher at a physics lab in

Switzerland. The issue that Berners-Lee was trying to overcome was the need for physicists to share research documents in an efficient manner with other physicists around the world. His solution was outlined in a proposal he wrote in 1989. Berners-Lee outlined his conception of a system that included three major elements: (1) HTML to develop documents, (2) HTTP to transmit the created documents, and (3) a software program (a browser) that would receive, interpret, and display data. A key concept of the proposal was consistency. Berners-Lee wanted to design a system that would allow users to access information no matter what type of computer they were using.

A working prototype of this system was not realized until early 1991 when it was used on a single Web server in Switzerland at the physics laboratory (CERN) where Berners-Lee worked. In late 1991, this Web server was made accessible to the general public. By the end of 1992, there were more than fifty Web servers available throughout the world. Most were located at research centers and major universities. The number of public servers grew to approximately 24 million by 2002!

## LOOKING INTO THE CRYSTAL BALL: THE FUTURE OF THE WEB

Predicting the future of the Web is a difficult task, if not an impossible one. Despite this, we will step into our prognosticator shoes to make a few predictions. Rest assured our predictions are based on research and expert opinions.

One prediction that can be made with a great deal of certainty is that with each passing day, more and more people will gain access to the Web. Various studies and surveys indicate that the number of current Web users is anywhere between 500 to 600 million worldwide. This number has increased significantly over the past five years as Internet connectivity has improved. However, despite this increase, there still exist inequities to Web access throughout the World (see Chapter 4 for a discussion of these inequities). Inequities exist in the United States as well. Based on these statistics, we can make a reasonable assumption that many of your students will have access to the Web, and most likely will have used it numerous times before entering your classroom. The Web will be something that they (and their parents) will expect to have incorporated into the classroom.

Another prediction regarding the Web deals with bandwidth. As described earlier, bandwidth deals with the amount of digital information that can be sent or received over a given time. As advances are made to the mediums and methods by which digital data is transmitted, the types of activities that can be accomplished on the Web will change.

Increased bandwidth will allow for larger amounts of information to be transmitted more quickly, thus allowing for real-time communication and collaboration to take place on a regular basis. A musician in Detroit will be able to record music with other musicians who are located in Los Angeles. Doctors will control robotic instruments over the Web to perform surgery on patients who may be thousands of miles away. Students who cannot make it to a classroom for various reasons will be able to collaborate with other students and their teacher through the Web. The *Internet2* is a large scale project that is working on making these scenarios a reality. The Internet2 is a high-bandwidth Internet network that is a collaborative effort spear-headed by major universities, the federal government, and corporations.

# Resource B

## *Try Spinning a Web Page!* Blackline Master

The *Try Spinning a Web Page!* worksheet is designed to help develop an understanding of how HTML works and how easy it can be to create simple Web pages. We recommend using this as part of a formal workshop on Web basics or as part of informal professional development.

## TRY SPINNING A WEB PAGE!

Making a Web page using HTML is easier than you may think. Follow the five steps listed here to create and view a Web page that you create on your computer.

1. Activate a simple word-processing application like Notepad, Wordpad, Simpletext, or TextEdit (virtually every Windows-based or Macintosh computer has one of these on it).

2. On the blank page (new file), type the following:

   ```
   <HTML>

   <HEAD>

   <TITLE>

   My Page

   </TITLE>

   </HEAD>

   <BODY>

   This is my <b>Web page!</b> It is the beginning
   of many wonderful pages to come.

   <p>

   This is a new paragraph. I can make a new
   paragraph any time I wish by inserting a
   paragraph tag.

   </BODY>

   </HTML>
   ```

3. Save the file as *my_page.html* (keep in mind the rules about proper file names as discussed in Chapter 3). If you save it to your desktop it will be particularly easy to locate in Step 4.

4. Open any browser on your computer (e.g. Internet Explorer, Netscape, Safari). From your browser, select "Open File" (usually found in the "File" pull-down menu) and choose the file you have just created (you will probably select "browse" to find the file on your computer).

5. You should now see your Web page displayed in your browser!

# References

American Library Association. (2005). *Standards and guidelines.* Chicago: Association of College and Research Libraries. Retrieved July 16, 2007, from http://www.ala.org/ala/acrl/acrlstandards/standardsguidelines.htm

Bare, J., & Meek, A. (1998). *Issue brief: Internet access in public schools, February 1998* (E.D. TABS Publication No. NCES 98–031). Washington, DC: U.S. Government Printing Office.

Barrows, H. S. (1996). Problem-based learning in medicine and beyond: A brief overview. In L. Wilkerson & W. H. Gijselaers (Eds.), *Bringing problem-based higher education: Theory and practice: New directions for teaching and learning* (pp. 3–12). San Francisco: Jossey-Bass.

Berners-Lee, T. (1998). *The world wide web: A very short personal history.* Retrieved July 18, 2006, from http://www.w3.org/People/Berners-Lee/ShortHistory

Berners-Lee, T., & Feschetti, M. (2000). *Weaving the web: The original design and ultimate destiny of the world wide web, by its inventor.* New York: HarperCollins.

Bray, M., Brown, A., & Green, T. (2004). *Technology and the diverse learner.* Thousand Oaks, CA: Corwin Press.

Brown, A., Green, T., & Zatz, D. (2001). Guidelines for multimedia production projects. *Educause Quarterly, 24*(4), 26–29.

California Department of Education. (2000). *History-social science content standards for California public schools (kindergarten through grade 12).* Sacramento, CA: Author.

California State Board of Education. (2005). *Content standards.* Retrieved June 29, 2007, from http://www.cde.ca.gov/be/st/ss/

Connell, B. R., Jones, M., Mace, R., Mueller, J., Mullick, A., Ostroff, E., et al. (1997). *The principles of universal design.* Raleigh: North Carolina State University, The Center for Universal Design. Retrieved August 25, 2006, from http://www.design.ncsu.edu/cud/about_ud/udprinciples.htm

Ellis, A. K. (2001). *Research on educational innovations* (3rd ed.). Larchmont, NY: Eye on Education.

Green, T. (2001). Teaching students to critically evaluate web pages. *The Clearing House, 75*(1), 32–34.

Green, T., & Brown, A. (2002a). *Multimedia production in the classroom: A guide to development and evaluation.* Thousand Oaks, CA: Corwin Press.

Green, T., & Brown, A. (2002b). Student-generated multimedia projects in the classroom. *Multimedia Schools, 9*(4), 20–25.

Hebert, E. A. (2001). *The power of portfolios: What children can teach us about learning and assessment.* San Francisco: Jossey-Bass.

International Society for Technology in Education. (2000). *National educational technology standards for students: Connecting curriculum and technology.* Eugene, OR: Author.

International Society for Technology in Education. (2004). *Technology foundation standards for all students.* Eugene, OR: Author. Retrieved June 29, 2007, from http://cnets.iste.org/students/s_stands.html

International Society for Technology in Education. (2007). *National educational technology standards for students* (2nd ed.). Eugene, OR: Author.

Johnson, D. W., & Johnson, R. T. (1999). *Learning together and alone: Cooperative, competitive, and individualistic learning* (5th ed.). Boston: Allyn & Bacon.

Kelly, M. G. (2002). *National Educational Technology Standards for Teachers: Preparing teachers to use technology.* Eugene, OR: International Society for Technology in Education.

Liu, J. (1996). *Understanding www search tools.* Retrieved July 18, 2007, from http://www.uni-mannheim.de/users/bibsplit/search_tools/body.html

McKenzie, J. (1995). *Beyond technology: Questioning, research, and the information literate school.* FNO.org. Retrieved July 18, 2007, from http://fno.org.beyond tech.html

Meyer, D. H., & Rose, M. (2002). *Teaching every student in the digital age: Universal design for learning.* Alexandria, VA: Association for Supervision & Curriculum Development.

National Telecommunications and Information Administration. (2000). *Falling through the net: Toward digital inclusion.* Washington, DC: Author.

New Jersey State Department of Education. (2004). *New Jersey core curriculum content standards.* Retrieved June 29, 2007, from http://www.state.nj.us/njded/cccs/

Niederst, J. (2001). *Learning web design: A beginner's guide to html, graphics and beyond* (2nd ed.). Sebastopol, CA: O'Reilly.

Prensky, M. (2001). Digital natives, digital immigrants. *On the Horizon, 5*(9), 1–5.

Piper, P. (2000). Better read that again: Web hoaxes and misinformation. *Searcher, 8*(8), 40–49. Retrieved July 18, 2007, from http://www.infotoday.com/searcher/sep00/piper.htm

Rawe, J. (2006). How safe is Myspace? *Time, 168*(1), 34–36.

Reigeluth, C. (Ed.). (1983). *Instructional-design theories and models: An overview of their current status.* Hillsdale, NJ: Lawrence Erlbaum.

Richardson, W. (2006). *Blogs, wikis, podcasts, and other powerful web tools for classrooms.* Thousand Oaks, CA: Corwin Press.

Sharan, S. (Ed.). (1999). *Handbook of cooperative learning methods.* New York: Praeger.

Shea, V. (1994). *Netiquette.* San Francisco: Albion.

Slavin, R. (1994). *Cooperative learning: Theory, research, and practice.* Boston: Allyn & Bacon.

Stepien, W. J., & Gallagher, S. A. (1993). Problem-based learning: As authentic as it gets. *Educational Leadership, 50*(7), 25–28.

U.S. Department of Education. (2004). *Toward a new golden age in American education: How the internet, the law, and today's students are revolutionizing expectations.* National Education Technology Plan. Washington, DC: Author.

USC, Anneberg School Center for the Digital Future. (2004). *Ten years, ten trends. The digital future report: Surveying the digital future, year four.* Retrieved June 29, 2007, from http://www.digitalcenter.org/downloads/DigitalFutureReport-Year4-2004.pdf

Warnings about social-networking sites: College orientation programs caution freshmen about these online resources. (2006, August 4). *eSchool News.*

Web-Based Education Commission. (2000, December). *The power of the internet for learning: Moving from promise to practice.* Report to the President and the Congress of the United States. Retrieved June 29, 2007, from http://www.ed.gov/offices/AC/WBEC/FinalReport/index.html

# Index

**CORWIN PRESS**

The Corwin Press logo—a raven striding across an open book—represents the union of courage and learning. Corwin Press is committed to improving education for all learners by publishing books and other professional development resources for those serving the field of PreK–12 education. By providing practical, hands-on materials, Corwin Press continues to carry out the promise of its motto: **"Helping Educators Do Their Work Better."**